WITHDRAWN
AUGUSTANA COLLEGE
LIBRARY

THE THINK ALOUD METHOD

A practical guide to modelling cognitive processes

THE THINK ALOUD METHOD

A practical guide to modelling cognitive processes

Maarten W. van Someren
Yvonne F. Barnard
Jacobijn A.C. Sandberg

Department of Social Science Informatics
University of Amsterdam

ACADEMIC PRESS
Harcourt Brace & Company, Publishers
London Boston San Diego New York
Sydney Tokyo

ACADEMIC PRESS LIMITED
24-28 Oval Road
LONDON NW1 7DX

U.S. Edition Published by
ACADEMIC PRESS INC.
San Diego, CA 92101

This book is printed on acid free paper

Copyright © 1994 ACADEMIC PRESS LIMITED

All rights reserved

No part of this book may be reproduced or transmitted in any form or by any means, electronic or mechanical including photocopying, recording, or any information storage and retrieval system without permission in writing from the publisher.

A catalogue record of this book is available from the British Library

ISBN 0-12-714270-3

Printed in Great Britain by Hartnolls Limited, Bodmin, Cornwall.

Contents

1 Thinking aloud   **1**
    1.1   A first impression   1
    1.2   Theories of cognitive processes in problem-solving   8
    1.3   Building knowledge-based systems   9
    1.4   Overview of this book   11

2 Studying the content of cognitive processes   **13**
    2.1   Introduction   13
    2.2   Cognitive processes in problem-solving   13
    2.3   Observation methods   15
    2.4   Structured techniques   16
    2.5   Verbal reports   19
        2.5.1   The verbal reporting process   19
        2.5.2   Retrospection   20
        2.5.3   Introspection   22
        2.5.4   Questions and prompting   22
        2.5.5   Dialogue observation   23
    2.6   Differences between methods   24
    2.7   Think aloud protocols   25
    2.8   Combining methods   26

3 The think aloud method   **29**
    3.1   Introduction   29
    3.2   History of the think aloud method   29
    3.3   Selecting subjects   34
        3.3.1   Criteria for selecting subjects   34
        3.3.2   Experts as subjects   34
        3.3.3   Differences in verbalization skills   35
    3.4   Selecting problems   36
    3.5   Summary   37

	3.6	Overview of the analysis of think aloud protocols	37

4 Practical procedures in obtaining think aloud protocols — 41
- 4.1 Introduction 41
- 4.2 Setting 41
- 4.3 Instructions 42
- 4.4 Warming up 43
- 4.5 Behaviour of the experimenter and prompting 44
- 4.6 Recording 44
- 4.7 Transcription of the protocol 44
- 4.8 Review 48

5 Building models of problem-solving — 49
- 5.1 Introduction 49
- 5.2 Modelling cognitive processes 49
- 5.3 The form of models of cognitive processes 51
- 5.4 Procedural models and explanation of human behaviour 53
- 5.5 Building models 54
- 5.6 Task analysis 55
  - 5.6.1 The construction of a task analysis 55
  - 5.6.2 Example: task analysis of solving arithmetic word problems 57
  - 5.6.3 Example: task analysis of architectural design 63
  - 5.6.4 The role of task analysis 63
- 5.7 Theories of problem-solving 65
  - 5.7.1 The role of psychological theories 65
  - 5.7.2 Example: psychological theories on solving arithmetic word problems 67
  - 5.7.3 Example: psychological theories on problem-solving in architectural design 67
- 5.8 Psychological model 68
  - 5.8.1 The construction of psychological models 68
  - 5.8.2 Example: a psychological model of solving arithmetic word problems 69
  - 5.8.3 Example: a psychological model of architectural design 72
- 5.9 Dimensions of models 74
- 5.10 On the boundaries of task analysis and model construction . . 76

6 Languages for task analysis and psychological modelling — 79
6.1 Introduction — 79
6.2 A conceptual modelling language — 81
6.2.1 CPML — 81
6.2.2 Domain layer — 82
6.2.3 Inference layer — 84
6.2.4 Task layer — 87
6.2.5 Example: a CPML model of architectural design — 90
6.2.6 Concluding remarks — 95
6.3 Pseudo programming language — 96
6.4 Problem Behaviour Graph and production rule systems — 98
6.4.1 Problem Behaviour Graph (PBG) — 98
6.4.2 Example: part of a PBG model of architectural design — 99
6.4.3 Production rules — 101
6.4.4 Extensions of production rules — 104
6.4.5 Problem Behaviour Graphs, production rule systems and human memory — 106
6.5 Programming languages — 109
6.6 Using a language or adapting it — 111
6.7 Differences between languages — 112

7 Analysing the protocols — 115
7.1 Introduction — 115
7.2 The role of protocols as data in research — 117
7.3 Transcription and segmentation — 117
7.4 Coding scheme and verbalization theory — 118
7.4.1 Introduction — 118
7.4.2 Constructing a coding scheme — 119
7.4.3 Grain size and aggregation — 120
7.4.4 Special coding categories — 120
7.4.5 Coding form — 121
7.4.6 Example: a coding scheme for architectural design — 121
7.4.7 Verbalization theory — 122
7.4.8 Example of a verbalization theory — 123
7.4.9 Methodological requirements for the coding scheme — 124
7.5 Coding procedures — 125
7.5.1 Introduction — 125
7.5.2 Aggregation — 125
7.5.3 Coding — 125
7.5.4 Rating protocols or protocol fragments — 126

	7.6	Intercoder reliability	126
	7.7	Comparing the coded protocols with the models	131
	7.7.1	Introduction	131
	7.7.2	Comparing protocols with procedural models	131
	7.7.3	Issues in quantifying the fit	133
	7.7.4	Comparing sets of protocols	134
	7.8	Computer support tools for analysis	134
	7.8.1	Introduction	134
	7.8.2	Indexing tools	135
	7.8.3	An implemented model as tool	135
	7.9	Reporting the results of protocol analysis	135

8 Examples   139

8.1		Introduction	139
8.2		Solving physics problems	139
	8.2.1	Introduction	139
	8.2.2	An example problem	140
	8.2.3	The model of advanced problem solving	140
	8.2.4	Design of the experiments	143
	8.2.5	A protocol	144
	8.2.6	Coding the protocol	146
	8.2.7	Results	148
	8.2.8	The sequence of tasks	149
	8.2.9	The completeness of the model	149
	8.2.10	The level of detail of the model	150
	8.2.11	Conclusion	150
8.3		Explaining novice errors in computer programming	150
	8.3.1	Introduction	150
	8.3.2	The model	150
	8.3.3	Design of the study	152
	8.3.4	An analysed protocol	152
	8.3.5	Conclusion	154
8.4		Acquisition of medical knowledge	155
	8.4.1	Example: a medical diagnosis task	155
	8.4.2	Knowledge structures	156
	8.4.3	The problem-solving process	158
	8.4.4	Alternative models	160
	8.4.5	Predicted and actual protocol	161
	8.4.6	Results	164
	8.4.7	Conclusion	165

A	**Exercises**	**167**
	A.1 Exercise 1: collecting verbal data	167
	A.2 Exercise 2: applicability of the think aloud method	168
	A.3 Exercise 3: task analysis and model construction	168
	A.3.1 Introduction	168
	A.3.2 Example problem	169
	A.3.3 Suggestions for task analysis and psychological model	170
	A.3.4 Exercise	172
	A.4 Exercise 4: knowledge acquisition	172
	A.5 Exercise 5: physics problem solving	173
B	**Instructions for two problem-solving tasks**	**175**
	B.1 Task 1: waterjug problems	175
	B.2 Task 2: improving technical devices	175
C	**Protocols of 'learning word meanings'**	**177**
D	**Analysing expert problem-solving**	**185**
	D.1 Case description	185
	D.2 Protocol	186
E	**Coding scheme architectural design**	**193**
F	**Protocol of novice problem-solving in physics**	**199**
	Bibliography	**203**
	Index	**207**

Preface

This book gives a detailed description of the *think aloud method*. The think aloud method consists of asking people to think aloud while solving a problem and analysing the resulting verbal protocols. This method has applications in psychological and educational research on cognitive processes but also for the knowledge acquisition in the context of building knowledge-based computer systems. In many cases the think aloud method is a unique source of information on cognitive processes. In this book we present the method in detail with examples.

This book is intended for two types of readers: social scientists who want to use the think aloud method for research on cognitive processes and knowledge engineers who want to use the method for knowledge acquisition. To make the book readable for both audiences, it contains short introductions to issues that are basic knowledge for one readership, but that are not part of the standard knowledge in the other community. We have included introductory sections on those topics that are relevant for both communities. As a result the book presupposes almost no specific knowledge but it is written for readers who are basically familiar with one of the two major application areas of the think aloud method: research on cognitive processes and knowledge acquisition. The role of the think aloud method (and related techniques) is explained separately for psychological research and for knowledge acquisition. The book discusses the aspects of computer models that are directly associated with the think aloud method but not programming techniques.

This book has grown out of a long tradition at the University of Amsterdam. The tradition started in the 1930s with Otto Selz who used the think aloud method to study the creative reasoning processes. In the 1940s A.D. de Groot used the method in his famous study of thought processes in chess. In the 1960s and 1970s Jan Elshout and his colleagues used the method in detailed process studies of cognitive skills that were related to general intelligence. In this period Elshout also designed the first university course in which the method was taught. Many of the ideas presented in this book originate from this work. Bob Wielinga introduced techniques for computational modelling into the course and the method. This book is based directly on material used in a course on the think aloud method as it is taught at the University of Amsterdam. We hope to provide a practical guide to all who like to use the method in research or teach the method in a course.

Acknowledgments

The authors are grateful to all students who commented on earlier drafts of this text. Furthermore we like to thank Ronald Hamel and Wouter Jansweijer who allowed us to use their work on architectural design and on physics problem-solving as illustrative material in this book and who gave many useful comments on earlier drafts. Finally we thank the Department of Social Science Informatics at the Faculty of Psychology of the University of Amsterdam for the time and resources that allowed us to write this book.

The protocol texts of architects in Chapter 1, Figure 5.2 and the coding scheme in Appendix E were adapted with permission of R. Hamel: Het denken van de architect, AHA Books, 1990, distributed by Staatsdrukkerij en Uitgeverij (SDU), 's Gravenhage.

The protocols of physics problem solving and the description of the model of physics problem solving in Chapter 8 were adapted with permission of W.H.N. Jansweijer: PDP: Een benadering vanuit de kunstmatige intelligentie van probleemoplossen en leren door doen in een semantisch rijk domein, 1988, PhD thesis, University of Amsterdam.

Chapter 1

Thinking aloud

1.1 A first impression

Suppose that you want to understand the design process of architects, the knowledge that they use, the cognitive actions that they take and the strategies they employ. How would you go about this? One obvious possibility is to ask some architects how they design a building. Interestingly enough, they will not find this an easy question to answer. They are used to *do* their job, not to *explain* it. If they do try to tell you how they go about their design work, it is quite possible that their account of it will be incomplete or even incorrect, because they construct this account from memory. They may be inclined to describe the design process neatly in terms of the formal design methods that they acquired during their professional training, whereas the real design process deviates from these methods. Psychologists have demonstrated that such accounts are not very reliable. Another possibility is to look at the architects' designs and at their intermediate sketches. However, now you are looking at the *products* of the thought processes of these architects, and not at the *thought processes* themselves. What is needed are more direct data on the ongoing thinking processes during working on a design. If you want to know how they arrive at their designs, what they think, what is difficult for them and what is easy, how they reconcile conflicting demands, a different research method is needed.

A good method in this situation is to ask architects to work on a design and to instruct them to think aloud. What they say is recorded and used as data for analysis of the design process. This is a very direct method to gain insight in the knowledge and methods of human problem-solving. The speech and writings are called spoken and written *protocols*. In this book we will describe a method for systematically collecting and analysing such think aloud protocols. This method can be used by psychologists and other social scientists who want to know more about cognitive processes. It is also an important method for knowledge engineers whose goal is to build a knowledge-based computer system on the basis of human expertise.

First let us start with an example of a think aloud protocol of an architect who is engaged in a design task. The example is taken from a study by Ronald Hamel (1990) on the process of architectural design. Hamel was interested in the thought processes of architects. Many architects believe that their reasoning process is an unstructured flow of ideas that at some point converges to a design. Hamel's hypothesis was that the thought process may have a structure that is similar to that of other problem solving processes studied by psychologists. He started his research with the development of a descriptive, psychological model of architectural design.

Hamel defined a design task and found architects who were prepared to perform the design task while thinking aloud. The task was to design a facility for children up to the age of 16. The facility had to consist of a simple building in which all kinds of indoor activities can take place, two playing grounds, one for small children and one for children between 6 and 10 years old, and a sports field. The architects involved in the study were provided with descriptions, maps and photographs of the specific location of the proposed facility. They were asked to produce an initial design for the facility, to draw a plan and to make sketches taking different angles. They could use several drawing materials and could ask the researcher for more information. They were allowed to work on this task for two hours. The architects were asked to think aloud, and their utterances were tape-recorded.

One of Hamel's ideas was that the design process would consist of a cycle of the following steps: analysing the current problem, proposing a solution, implementing a solution, evaluating the solution.

Here follows a fragment of a verbatim protocol. This fragment starts at the point where the architect has decided to design an inner court. Now he is thinking about the problem how to make this court an interesting playground for the children.

```
1:   then you find there, er, something like a place for parents
     to sit
2:   so ... a bench
3:   water they will probably want
4:   would you want that like a tap or would you ...
```

5: want that like something they could play with some more a kind of ...
6: tub, er, yes
7: a water tub they can just fit their bare feet into or so
8: but that is going to make a mess in winter of course ...
9: so the question is whether that's what you want
10: a bit of a mess it will be
11: er, that is lovely in summer naturally
12: but maybe we can with er do something with that shack
13: water I'll just put tap [notes 'tap']
14: what children of course
15: what what what is much handier
16: [sketches water tub]
17: maybe something, er, where water comes out of, er,
18: and that you turn off in winter
19: but then it does not trouble you
20: and then it may run into here somewhere
21: then they can still mess about ... with water
22: then they can play with this
23: that just comes it slowly drips out of it or so
24: then they'll get dripping wet in summer
25: and then they can get around this
26: plus I'll just take that water tub
27: for maybe we'll find something that, er,
28: we'll do that later
29: [notes 'water tub']
30: that that we'll find something which gives you
31: fun with it in summer
32: and no trouble in winter
33: for that's what it is about...
34: the best would be of course if the roof could come off the building [laughs]
35: no trouble in winter but well
36: then you'll have these kids up on that roof again ...
37: and that is fine
38: but naturally that is a bit dangerous for certain age groups

From his initial model of the problem-solving process, Hamel developed a coding scheme which described in detail what kinds of actions belong to each category identified in the model. Next he categorized protocol fragments in terms of these actions. This made it possible to compare the design process of a particular architect with the model of the design process. For example, at the beginning of the protocol the architect is elaborating the area around the building. This can be used as a playground for children, which in turn requires objects to play with. He suggests a water tap, but evaluates this as not very good for playing. He replaces this idea by a water tub which leads to a long evaluation. This indicates that there is actually an underlying structure in the thought process. Cycles of analysing the current problem, proposing a solution, implementing a solution, and evaluating the solution were clearly present in the protocols.

Note that the protocol gives information about the architect's reasoning that could not be obtained by simply looking at the resulting design. The protocol gives data about strategies and the knowledge that the architect uses to construct a design, data about lines of reasoning that were abandoned at some point and so on.

Both the structure of the problem-solving process and the results of problem-solving steps that appear in the protocol can be used as a basis for a knowledge-based computer system that performs or supports an architectural design. For example, it provides several arguments that can be used to evaluate whether a water tub is an appropriate solution to a sub-problem in architectural design.

Hamel's study of architectural design focused on a particular aspect of the reasoning process: the overall structure of the reasoning process. His study involved competent problem solvers because the goal was the study of competent design. A different goal may be the study of the behaviour of less competent problem solvers. In psychology one often wants to explain errors or inefficient problem-solving behaviour. One task that has been studied extensively is the solving of arithmetic word problems. Consider for example the problem:

A father, a mother and their son are 80 years old together. The father is twice as old as the son. The mother has the same age as the father. How old is the son?

If we present this problem to two students, and if they both give the correct solution, then we can not just assume that their problem-solving processes are the same. Below we show two think aloud protocols taken from two psychology students who both solved the problem given above.

Student 1:

1: a father, a mother and their son are together 80 years old
2: the father is twice as old as the son
3: the mother is as old as the father
4: how old is the son?
5: well, that sounds complicated
6: let's have a look
7: I just call them F, M and S
8: F plus M plus S is 80
9: F is 2 times S
10: and M equals F
11: what do we have now?
12: three equations and three unknowns
13: so S ...
14: 2 times F plus S is 80
15: so 4 times S plus S is 80
16: so 5 times S is 80
17: S is 16
18: yes, that is possible
19: so father and mother are 80 minus 16
20: 64
21: er ... 32.

Student 2:

1: father, mother and son are together 80 years old
2: how is that possible?
3: if such a father is 30 and mother too
4: then the son is 20
5: no, that is not possible
6: if you are 30, you cannot have a son of 20
7: so they should be older
8: about 35, more or less
9: let's have a look
10: the father is twice as old as the son
11: so if he is 35 and the son 17
12: no, that is not possible
13: 36 and 18
14: then the mother is
15: 36 plus 18 is 54

```
16: 26 ...
17: well, it might be possible
18: no, then she should have had a child when she was 9
19: oh, no
20: no, the father should, the mother should be older
21: for example 30
22: but then I will not have 80
23: 80 minus 30, 50
24: then the father should be nearly 35 and the son nearly 18
25: something like that
26: let's have a look, where am I?
27: the father is twice ...
28: the mother is as old as the father
29: oh dear
30: my mother, well not my mother
31: but my mother was 30 and my father nearly 35
32: that is not possible
33: if I make them both 33
34: then I have together 66
35: then there is for the son ... 24
36: no, that is impossible
37: I don't understand it anymore
38: 66, ..., 80
39: no, wait, the son is 14
40: almost, ... the parents are too old
41: 32, 32, 64, 16, yes
42: the son is 16 and the parents 32, together 80
```

When we compare these two protocols, we see two very different problem-solving processes. The first student treats the problem as mathematical equation and solves it straightforwardly. The second student uses another strategy. He starts with a guess: the father is 30 years old. He evaluates the result by using knowledge about reasonable age differences between parents and children. Then he forms a new estimation, and evaluates it again. The two students give the same answer, but they use a very different solving strategy. The think aloud protocols give a clear insight in how they reach the solution. The protocols show clearly how the students solve the problem step by step. The second protocol also shows where this student encounters difficulties and when he gets confused.

This illustrates how think aloud protocols can provide data about both sophisticated and less sophisticated cognitive processes that are difficult to obtain by other means. Therefore it is an essential method for areas such as cognitive psychology, educational science and knowledge acquisition. The protocols given above may give the impression that protocols in general are easy to understand. This is not always the case. Below we give a protocol that is more typical than those above. This fragment comes from a protocol by a child (12 years old) who solves the following problem:

Irene has 6 sweets less than Suzanne. Diana has 5 more than Suzanne. How many sweets does Irene have less than Diana?

```
1:  so Suzanne has 6 more than Irene
2:  and Diana has 5 more than Suzanne
3:  so Suzanne comes first
4:  because Suzanne has some 5, er, 6
5:  but Diana has 5 more, even more
6:  so altogether 11
7:  but less is asked here
8:  how many does Irene have less than Suzanne
9:  then you subtract that
10: Diana, Suzanne, Irene
```

At this point the experimenter intervenes and says:
If Diana has the most sweets and Irene has the fewest sweets, then how can it be that Irene has only one less than Diana?

```
11: [reads the problem again]
12: I don't understand it ...
13: Irene has something of which Suzanne has 6 more
14: Diana has 5 more than Suzanne
15: so something must be added
16: and then something must be subtracted
17: if I knew how many Suzanne had
18: Suzanne has 11, I think
19: Diana has 5 more than Suzanne
20: [pause] 10, I think
21: how many does Irene have less than Diana
22: I think 10
23: [gives up]
```

This protocol illustrates that it may be hard to understand think aloud protocols, even when they concern relatively simple tasks, such as this arithmetic word problem. For now, we shall leave the interpretation of this protocol to the reader. We return to it in Chapter 5.

The examples above gave a first impression of the think aloud method. This method consists of (a) collecting think aloud protocols like those above and (b) analysing the protocols to obtain a model of the cognitive processes that take place during problem solving or to test the validity of a model that is derived from a psychological theory. Protocols are collected by instructing people to solve one or more problems while saying 'what goes through their head', stating directly what they think. In studies on cognition, verbal protocols are used as raw data about cognitive processes. Such protocols require substantial interpretation and analysis to see their implications for process theories of problem-solving. The other main application of the think aloud method is to collect expert knowledge which may be used as the basis for a computer system. This book introduces both types of application of protocol analysis for those readers who are not familiar with either cognitive psychology or knowledge acquisition for computer systems. Before we continue with a more detailed description of the think aloud method, we will elaborate on the role this method plays in psychology and in knowledge acquisition for knowledge-based computer systems.

1.2 Theories of cognitive processes in problem-solving

Problem-solving means answering a question for which one does not directly have an answer available. This can be because the answer cannot be directly retrieved from memory but must be constructed from information that is available in memory or that can be obtained from the environment (for example, the givens of the problem or extra information that can be requested). Another possibility is that finding the answer involves exploring possible answers none of which is immediately recognized as the solution to a problem. Problem-solving then means that new information must be inferred from givens and knowledge in memory to accept or reject possible answers. Most problem-solving involves a combination of these two types of reasoning: constructing solutions and constructing justifications of these solutions.

Problem-solving is the cognitive process to which the think aloud method is applied most frequently. It can also be applied to other processes that produce intermediate thoughts that can be verbalized. For example, *learning* processes in the context of problem-solving are studied by Anzai & Simon (1979). In this study the think aloud method is used to identify changes in the knowledge during repeated problem-solving on a single task (in addition to the way in which the problem-solving task itself is performed).

The think aloud method can be used to investigate differences in problem-solving abilities between people, differences in difficulty between tasks, effects of instruction and other factors that have an effect on problem-solving. Some theories under investigation concern fairly detailed aspects of the processes involved in problem-solving. Their aim is to explain almost every step taken by the problem solver. Other theories employ more general properties of problem-solving processes and use more global properties of people. For example, pupils' performance on an arithmetic test potentially can be explained from general intelligence, from some particular type of intelligence, from the general performance level at school, from specific performance at arithmetic, or even from the detailed knowledge that the student had at the time when she made the test. The think aloud method is only relevant if properties of the solution *process* are relevant to the theory. The think aloud method is a means to validate or construct theories of cognitive processes, in particular of problem-solving.

1.3 Building knowledge-based systems

Protocol analysis is not only used for the scientific study of cognitive processes, but also for the construction of knowledge-based systems. For those readers who are unfamiliar with the area of knowledge-based systems (or 'expert systems') we give a brief introduction. Knowledge-based computer systems are computer programs that perform tasks that normally are performed by human experts. These systems are based on the knowledge of human experts in a certain area on how to perform a specific task. Examples of such tasks are medical diagnosis, monitoring production processes, giving advice about legal conflicts and giving advice about the stock market. If human experts are available, their knowledge will be the basis of the system. This knowledge must then be acquired from the expert and represented in the computer system. Just as in the case of psychological or educational research, an obvious way to obtain the knowledge is to ask experts how they perform a task, which knowledge they use, etc. However, experience has shown that people are often unable to tell how they perform a task. Even worse, there is evidence that they may give false information. The think aloud method is a good way to avoid 'false' information and obtain direct data about the solution process that takes place when an expert solves a problem.

The most important characteristics of knowledge-based systems are the following:

Expert level performance: performance is comparable to the level reached by humans who are specialized in this task.
Narrow task domain: only a relatively small class of problems can be solved by the system. Usually these systems lack the knowledge required to solve a wide range of problems.
Explanation: the system can explain or justify its outcomes by displaying its reasoning and the knowledge on which this is based. To provide acceptable explanations, the system needs enough explicit knowledge about the task and therefore it must be more than just a table of rules relating problems to answers. The knowledge that is used to generate these explanations is usually based on the way in which human experts find the solution to a problem. This makes it necessary to acquire this knowledge.

Experts are the main source of the knowledge that is used to build the program. They are not the only source, of course, since relevant knowledge can also be found in textbooks, manuals and specialized literature. However, specific expertise that is acquired by one or more human experts in many years of experience with the task at hand is an essential ingredient here. Expert systems are often constructed for tasks for which expertise is rare and expensive. A goal of building a knowledge-based system can be to make expertise available to many people in an organization, or to an even wider audience. Note that the notion of 'expert' is relative here. Some 'experts' do by no means show perfect performance, but are only experts relative to most other people. For example, financial experts are not able to predict economic processes without making errors, nor are medical specialists able to diagnose diseases perfectly. They are just more knowledgeable than most other people.

The think aloud method is an element in the repertory of methods available to the *knowledge engineer* who acquires the knowledge for the system and who designs and sometimes implements the system. Collecting knowledge from an expert is called *knowledge elicitation*. Other elicitation techniques are for example interviewing, collecting problems that are presented to an expert and the expert's solution or systematically asking the expert to define important concepts in the domain.

Initially, knowledge-based systems were built in a very direct way: the knowledge engineer simply asked an expert how to find the solution to a problem and then used the expert's statements to program an initial version of the system. This method is called 'rapid prototyping', because it relies on quick construction of prototypes of the system. The prototype is used for the elicitation of new knowledge: it is demonstrated to the expert, who then criticizes and extends it, which leads to the second version of the system. This procedure is repeated until knowledge engineer and expert are more or less satisfied with the system.

This style of development is not adequate for the construction of larger systems, because constructing a new prototype from a previous version becomes increasingly difficult when the system becomes larger. Modern development methodologies (in particular KADS, see Schreiber et al., 1993) emphasize the need for a structured approach that begins with an analysis of the requirements for the system, including the required user interaction and an analysis of the expertise from which the system is to be built. This is done without constructing a program. The analysis is done on paper, in a special modelling language.

For example, in the context of medical diagnosis it is important to find a task that can be performed by a computer and that fits in the organizational structure. The data for the task must be available or it must be possible to feed them into the computer. It must be possible to separate the task for the future computer system from other tasks that are performed by people. For example, if the data that are needed for diagnosis must also be recorded in a medical file then it must be possible to avoid collecting these data twice. If only certain people are authorized to have access to patient data this has consequences for the system. If the data must be readily available during treatment of the patient and if it must be possible to update these data, this has consequences for the system. All such issues are dealt with by designing an *organization model* that defines the role of the future system in the organization with respect to other persons and departments in the organization.

Once a suitable task is identified, the knowledge required for performing this task must be acquired. This is where think aloud protocols can be used. In particular knowledge about the problem-solving *process* can be acquired in this way. Other sources and elicitation techniques are normally used to identify basic concepts and knowledge in the domain but as in psychological research, the think aloud method is one of the few techniques that give direct data about the reasoning process. This knowledge is represented in a structured format and is used as the basis for designing and implementing the computer system.

1.4 Overview of this book

The content of the rest of this book is structured as follows:

1. Collecting think aloud protocols
Chapter 2 describes techniques for studying problem-solving processes. This is used to sketch the main dimensions of these techniques and to characterize the position of the think aloud method among these techniques. Chapter 3 introduces the think aloud method and Chapter 4 the practical procedures for collecting verbal protocols.
2. Modelling cognitive processes
This issue is addressed in Chapter 5. Chapter 6 describes modelling languages that are often used for building models of problem-solving processes including computational languages.
3. Methodology for the analysis of think aloud protocols
This is presented in Chapter 7.
4. Examples
Chapter 8 gives some examples of the use of the think aloud method and this book ends with some exercises.

Literature

Hamel's research on architectural design is reported in Dutch in Hamel (1990). There are many overviews of psychological research on problem-solving. A good introduction is given by Anderson (1990). A good technically oriented introduction to knowledge-based systems is given by Jackson (1990). Schreiber et al. (1993) gives an overview of the KADS methodology, with an emphasis on modelling techniques. Overviews of elicitation techniques are given by Diaper (1989) and Meyer & Booker (1991). Recent developments are reported in the journals *Knowledge Acquisition* and *International Journal of Man-Machine Studies*.

Chapter 2

Studying the content of cognitive processes

2.1 Introduction

In this chapter we will describe several techniques for studying cognitive processes in problem-solving. We start with an introduction on these cognitive processes. Before we turn to the think aloud method, we will describe several other methods: the observation of problem-solving behaviour, structured techniques (especially in knowledge acquisition) and different forms of verbal reports. These methods are compared with each other. Then we will show the place of the think aloud method within the spectrum of other techniques regarding its use in psychology and in knowledge elicitation.

2.2 Cognitive processes in problem-solving

In this book we will concentrate on the cognitive processes in problem-solving. People frequently engage in problem-solving activities, professionally as well as privately. Problem-solving can be characterized as a cognitive process that is goal directed and requires effort and concentration of attention. The solution is not found directly in a single step but via intermediate reasoning steps, some of which may later appear useless or false. Some problems that people solve are well defined, for example mathematical equations, questions in a school physics examination, medical diagnosis problems in a standard setting. There are also examples of problem-solving activities in which the problem itself and its potential solution are not so well defined and where it is not so easy to evaluate the solutions in terms of correctness. Examples of these activities are: designing clothes, writing an article about the results of an experiment, selecting a new personnel member. Such activities require the solution of many smaller problems. In the case of clothes design, one has to find out what kinds of material may be used given the amount needed and the price allowed. In the case of writing an article, one has to find solutions to problems like when to start a new paragraph, how to phrase an idea, when to insert an illustration.

Problem-solving not only occurs in a professional or educational undertaking. In everyday life one has to solve a lot of problems. What shall we eat tonight, how much does a kilo of apples cost given the price of a pound, what is the most efficient route to the office, how to discuss marital problems with one's husband or wife? Sometimes you are well aware of the fact that you are trying to solve a problem, for example when you are trying to figure out how much something costs in a foreign currency. One is consciously trying to remember the exchange rate and performing the mathematical operations required. Sometimes problem-solving goes on without noticing, like when one decides which flowers to buy. You may not perceive your mental process as problem-solving. Still you are solving the problem of finding the flowers that harmonize with the colours of your furniture, that are in line with your partner's taste, that are not too high-priced, that will last for some time.

In all these examples the topic is the problem-solving *process* rather than the outcome of this process. One may want to study these problem-solving processes for many different reasons. Psychologists may be interested in the mechanisms underlying human reasoning, the causes of errors, the character and origin of differences in performance between people. Educational scientists may be interested in the effect of education or the difficulties that pupils experience when solving exercise problems. A knowledge engineer may want to understand how a person carries out a task, to be able to build a computer system that can do the same. As we shall show below, the aim you may have as researcher partly determines the nature of the procedure you follow, when using protocol analysis. In this chapter we discuss methods for collecting data about the content of cognitive processes, emphasizing their commonalities and differences. There are several research methods for gaining insight in aspects related to thinking and learning. We will illustrate the most important methods with the example of problem-solving processes that take place when a person solves a physics problem. The text of this problem is:

A container is closed by a piston. holds an ideal gas. The volume of the gas is 2 litres and the pressure is 120 kilopascals. By slowly moving the piston outwards, the volume is increased to 3 litres, while the temperature of the gas is kept constant. What is the pressure of the gas after the piston is moved?

This problem can be solved by making the assumption that 'slowly moving the piston outwards' means that energy is exchanged between the gas in the container and the environment. In that case the following relation holds between volume (V), pressure (P) and temperature (T) before (1) and after (2) moving the piston:

$$\frac{P_1 \times V_1}{T_1} = \frac{P_2 \times V_2}{T_2}$$

This relation is called *Boyle's Law*. In this case, the temperature is constant, which reduces this formula to:

$$P_1 \times V_1 = P_2 \times V_2 \text{ or: } P_2 = \frac{P_1 \times V_1}{V_2}$$

Substituting the data from the problem gives: $P_2 = \frac{120 \times 2}{3}$ which gives the answer: 80 kilopascals.

A psychologist or an educational scientist will be interested in, for example, differences between beginners and experts on this problem, in the cause of errors or in different strategies that people use to solve this problem. For example, novices tend to solve this problem 'backward'. They try to find a formula that has the *pressure* in it, try to 'fill' this with the other givens and see if this can solve the problem. A possible cause of errors for novice problem solvers lies in not checking if a formula applies to the situation described in the problem. Experts on the other hand tend to follow a forward reasoning strategy in the style of the explanation given above. Testing and exploring such hypotheses requires data on the problem solving process.

2.3 Observation methods

One class of methods is based on observation of problem-solving behaviour. The first, *product analysis*, uses the result of problem-solving. The solution to a problem may reflect aspects of the problem-solving behaviour. In the example above, the answer '800 kilopascals' would suggest an error in calculation. If notes are made during problem-solving, these provide additional information. However, these data do not tell us if the condition for applying the formula ('closed system') was checked or if the problem was solved 'backward' in novice style or 'forward' in expert style. More information about the problem-solving process can be obtained by observing the problem solving behaviour *concurrently* while it takes place. This is called *observation of behaviour*.

A researcher may observe the student's problem-solving behaviour. Does she give a solution immediately, does she make notes, does she hesitate often, what kind of literature does she use, which extra questions does she ask, etc? In the physics example the notes and the order in which they are taken can be observed and reconstructed. This will give more information than just observing the answer or the notes. However, very much information will not appear in the notes. Some tasks involve the manipulation of objects, for instance, an architect moving objects in a model. In the case of our student, she may first make a drawing of the situation and then look in a physics book for a physics law, or she may proceed the other way around. She may solve the problem in a short time span, or interrupt the process and work at the problem at some later time. She may seem to work cheerfully or sound desperate. Besides simple observation, special equipment may be used to observe properties that are not directly visible or audible. For example eye movements can be registered during problem-solving or even activity in various parts of the brain may be measured by special measurement techniques. These latter kind of measurements may provide data on what information is being focused on and processed at a certain moment.

Behavioural observations are registered as *action protocols*. If a person manipulates objects during problem-solving (for example when using a computer or another device) a behaviour trace can be stored. This is one of the few techniques that give access to data about the problem-solving process. The analysis of action protocols is very similar to that of think aloud protocols.

2.4 Structured techniques

Observation is an unstructured technique in the sense that it does not constrain the subjects' behaviour. The range of possible observations is therefore very broad. Another class of techniques that is used both in psychology and in knowledge acquisition uses predefined forms in which the subject should express his knowledge. This can be done in many ways, depending on the task for the subject and the purpose of the study. There is an infinite variety of possible formats. A possible format are questions with predefined answers from which one or more is selected. For example, we may ask a subject to solve the physics problem and ask *Did you use Boyle's Law? Yes/No* or *Did you check if the formula that you used to compute the answer was applicable? Yes/No* or *Did you solve the problem by reasoning backward from the question or forward from the givens of the problem? Forward/Backward*. Alternatively, we can ask questions in a general form such as *Do you normally check if a formula that you use to compute the answer is applicable before using it? Yes/No* or *Do you normally solve problems by reasoning backward from the question or forward from the givens of the problem? Forward/Backward*.

Note that some of these questions are difficult to answer and are likely to produce false answers. To obtain reliable results, the format has to correspond as closely as possible to what is known about the original cognitive process and the information that it involves, to avoid interpretation and distortion by the subject. Another factor that affects the quality of reports is the time interval between the process and the report. The questions in general form always ask about processes that took place over a longer period of time which will reduce the quality of the answers.

We give another example of a method using structured data that is taken from knowledge acquisition for expert systems: the Ariadna knowledge acquisition system (Morgoev, 1989). Ariadna is a computer-based elicitation system that collects data about a classification *process*. The problem-solving task is to classify an object by asking for information about the object. This can be, for example, a patient who must be diagnosed or an applicant who is to be classified as suitable or not for a job. Ariadna asks predefined questions but it allows the user some freedom in expressing the answers. Ariadna uses information provided by the user to generate new questions and it keeps track of questions that it should ask later. We give a sample dialogue between Ariadna and a medical expert. Ariadna plays two roles in the dialogue: that of an imaginary patient and of a dialogue director.

Ariadna: **What would be your first question?**
Expert: *Where is the pain?*
Ariadna: **What are the possible answers to this question?**
Expert: *Chest, left arm, right arm, head, left leg, right leg, stomach.*
Ariadna: **Suppose that the answer is 'chest'.**
          Which possible classifications are now still possible?
Expert: *Heart infarction, angina pectoris, functional complaints,*
          lung embolism, kidney dysfunction, arrhythmia.
Ariadna: **What would be your next question?**

Now Ariadna is back at its first step. This process continues until there are no more questions left. Ariadna assumes that the experts problem-solving consists of the following reasoning steps:

1. Ask for information (in this case symptoms and properties of a patient).
2. Use this information to find a set of possible classifications.

Initially a large set of possible classifications is generated, but gradually this set will become smaller when new information becomes available that excludes certain classifications.

When the user gives the possible answers to a question, Ariadna selects one (or the user can select one) but it also remembers that later on it should ask about the other possible answers. After some more questions the user will indicate that only one more class is still possible (or that there are no more useful questions). Now Ariadna will go back to an earlier point in the dialogue. It can return to the question above and ask the expert:

Ariadna: **Suppose that the answer to your question,** *'where is the pain?'* **was 'left arm'. Which possible classifications are now still possible?**

This process continues until the user stops it or until all possible answer patterns are discussed. In this way Ariadna collects a problem-solving trace that consists of the following elements:

- Information requests with their possible answers.
- Sets of possible classifications after each new piece of information.
- Possible classes after obtaining a series of answers.

Ariadna gives a structured solution trace and is able to actively prompt for new information in terms of this structure. The advantage over less structured techniques is that the information is well structured and that the active prompts make it likely that this information is reasonably complete. A disadvantage is that the information may not be complete in other aspects than the possible classifications. For example, the subject may reason about the possibilities and no trace is found of this (although the Ariadna system gives the subject the option to make notes during the session). Note that this particular method can only be used if the problem-solving task is of the 'classification dialogue' type as above. Ariadna could not be used to obtain data about physics problem-solving because the reasoning process in physics problem-solving has a completely different structure than the elimination of candidate diagnoses that is assumed by Ariadna. On the other hand, Ariadna does not require a strict format for the knowledge that is entered into the system.

In general the differences between structured and unstructured techniques are:

1. The structure makes it possible to generate directed requests for new information.
2. Structured information is 'closer' to a computer program, thus making it easier to build a program from it.
3. Structured techniques require the user to structure the information. This requires a kind of translation by the subject which distorts the information with respect to the cognitive process.

2.5 Verbal reports

2.5.1 The verbal reporting process

A final class of methods involves unstructured *verbal reports* of problem-solving. There are different ways in which verbal reports can be obtained. To appreciate the differences between these methods, a simple model of the verbal reporting process is useful. The model in Figure 2.1 is based on a simple model of the human cognitive system.

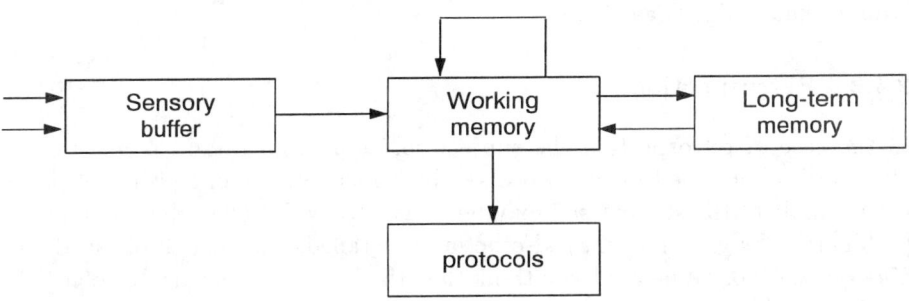

FIGURE 2.1: Memory model

Long-term memory (LTM) is the part where knowledge is stored more or less permanently. It takes some time to store information there and it can be retrieved later on to be used again. At the other end we find the sensory system that transforms information from the environment into an internal form. Working memory (WM) is the part where the currently 'active' information resides. In this model there are five processes:

1. **Perception:** Information flows from the sensory buffer into working memory.
2. **Retrieval:** Information is retrieved from long-term memory into working memory. It still exists in long-term memory but is activated into working memory.
3. **Construction:** New information is constructed from other information in working memory. For example, when solving the physics problem, someone may note that 'slowly moved piston' may in general refer to 'adiabatic process' and the resulting new association between these concepts is stored as a new object in working memory.
4. **Storage:** Stores information from working memory into long-term memory.
5. **Verbalization:** Information that is active in working memory is put into words. The output of this process is the spoken *protocol*.

Note that this model has several important implications for the meaning of verbal reports. One important point is that the information that can be verbalized is the content of working memory. This means that the content of long-term memory (the general knowledge) cannot be verbalized (unless it is somehow retrieved rather than used), nor can the cognitive architecture, the machinery, that applies the knowledge be verbalized. About these aspects only indirect knowledge is available.

2.5.2 Retrospection

In the case of retrospection the subject solves a problem and is questioned afterwards about the thought processes during the solving of a problem. So in the example of the student she may be asked: 'How did you solve the physics problem?' The questions may also be more detailed, like 'Which physical law did you use?', or 'When did you think that the problem was hard to solve?' It is also possible to record the problem-solving session on video and to review the video-tape together with the subject so she can give her interpretation of what happened when she looked into the textbook or made a note.

Retrospection may be difficult. It is not always easy to remember exactly what one did, especially if some time has passed after completion of the task. Sometimes even, one is not very aware of what one is doing. The physics student may have no conscious idea of how she calculated the filled-in formula. Another problem is that subjects may tend to present their thought processes as more coherent and intelligent than they originally were. Sometimes this is intentional, because people do not like to admit that they do not have the faintest idea of how to solve a problem considered as easy. So they will say: 'Well, I first stared at the problem statement and asked myself a few questions, like have I seen this problem before, do I know a procedure to solve this problem?' This may give the false impression of perfectly rational behaviour. In other cases, this kind of *post hoc* rationalizing happens unintentionally. If your behaviour was rather irrational to begin with, you may not remember it like that. Humans are just inclined to reconstruct events as more structured than they were originally. Their memory is guided by their knowledge of the result.

Psychologists have shown in many experiments that the data that are obtained by retrospection are not always valid (Nisbett & Wilson, 1979; Ericsson & Simon, 1993). People may not report thoughts that they have clearly had before and they will also report false memories: thoughts that they cannot have had at the time. Close examination of the conditions under which reports are unreliable has shown that all discrepancies were found in situations in which there was either a delay in time between the cognitive process and the report, or there was a question by the experimenter that required an interpretation rather than a direct report, ('Why did you do X instead of Y?'), or both. When asked for memories, explanations or motivations, people answer a question not from direct memory of the cognitive process but from an interpretation that can easily be influenced by expectations.

A classic example is an old study by Maier (1931). Subjects were brought into a room in which various objects were lying around and two ropes hang from the ceiling. Their task was to tie the ropes together. Because of the length of the ropes and the distance between them it was not possible to just take one, walk to the other and tie them together. After explaining the task, the experimenter gave two hints: he 'accidentally' touched one rope which made it swing back and forth a bit and, if a subject still failed to solve it after some time, the experimenter gave him a pair of scissors and told him: 'With the aid of this and no other object you can solve the problem'. In this case subjects found the solution (tie an object to the rope, swing it, walk to the other, pull it over and grab the swinging rope) much quicker than when the experimenter had not given a hint. Afterwards subjects were asked if they solved the problem 'as a whole', without intermediate steps leading to solution or that they gradually solved it in steps and they were also asked if they had noticed that the experimenter had touched the rope and if that had had any influence on their reasoning. Maier found that subjects who discovered the solution 'as a whole' reported that they had not noticed the cue or that they had not used it. The explanation for this is that from the subjects' perspective it must be highly unlikely that this would have had any effect, considering the time that they spent solving the problem (between several minutes and half an hour) and the sudden appearance of the solution. Yet, from the difference in solution time, one can conclude that the cue did have an effect.

The memory model explains why this is the case. Retrospection means that information must be retrieved from long-term memory and then verbalized. The disadvantage is that the retrieval process may not produce all information that actually appeared in working memory during the problem-solving process. What is worse, it is possible that information that was *not* actually in working memory is retrieved as if it was. After solving the physics problem, the solution will help to remember the steps that actually led to it. These are then easily reconstructed. However, odd and fruitless steps that occurred on the way are less likely to be retrieved.

2.5.3 Introspection

An alternative to retrospection is to instruct the subject to report not after completing the problem-solving task, but at intermediate points chosen by the subject. This is called introspection. In classic introspection, as used by psychologists in the 1920s and 1930s, the subject is also encouraged to give an accurate, complete and coherent report on a cognitive process. This may involve interpretation on the part of the subject, and the use of psychological terminology. As we shall see this technique is somewhere between retrospection and thinking aloud. The main difference with the think aloud method is that the latter requires *concurrent* verbalization and discourages interpretation on the part of the subject. As a result, introspective reports are more 'readable' than concurrent protocols but also more subject to memory errors and misinterpretations.

2.5.4 Questions and prompting

Another method implies actually interrupting the problem-solving process. The experimenter may ask questions during the problem-solving process or the subject may be prompted at given intervals to tell what he is thinking or doing. Examples are: 'Did you check if the formula applies here?', 'Why are you using this formula?', 'Does this problem remind you of another one?' or just 'What are you thinking of?', the latter being the most neutral prompt. By this method it is possible to explore specific aspects, selected by the experimenter, of the knowledge state of the subject at a given moment. The subject does not have the chance to 'smooth over' the answer as he may in the case of retrospection or to skip over it. The disadvantage of this method is that the problem-solving process is interrupted. The subject may have difficulty in taking up the thread. Prompts that require interpretation will affect the problem-solving process (see for example Chi et al., 1989; Ferguson-Hessler & de Jong, 1990; van Someren & Elshout, 1985). These prompts can be very similar to those proposed by educational scientists to improve problem solving performance and learning. It has been shown that asking questions about a text helps people to understand and remember the meaning.

In terms of the model of verbalization, prompting introduces additional cues in working memory that may lead to retrieval of spurious information from long-term memory and that may push current information out of working memory, disrupting the process. The advantage is that if the goal of the prompt is in working memory, it is more likely to be recorded than in any other method.

2.5.5 Dialogue observation

Some problem solving tasks naturally involve dialogues. Dialogues can be recorded on audio or video and the protocols can be used as verbal data about the process. These data are clearly different from individual verbal reports. However, dialogues have the advantage that they can be recorded under more natural circumstances than a think aloud session. We can distinguish *natural dialogues* from *induced dialogues*. A task can be adapted to induce dialogues. For example one can ask a subject to explain to someone else how to do the task. Our student might be asked to teach a junior student how to solve a kind of problem. This kind of instruction seems to work quite well with (young) children to whom the think aloud instruction is not very clear. Another possibility to enhance talkativeness is to get people to collaborate on a task. The task may be adjusted so that there is a real need for cooperation. For example, the task information may be divided between the collaborators (Barnard & Erkens, 1989). Such division really requires explicit exchange of information. Or they are asked to communicate solely by means of a connection between computer terminals (Sandberg *et al.*, 1988). In that case, the participants cannot support their utterances by gestures or facial expression, so they are obliged to be much more explicit in their statements. In these situations, the experimenter is enabled to study the interaction and is able to infer which information is used at what time. When people collaborate they will sometimes have differing opinions. Thus they are forced to give arguments, to clarify steps of their thinking processes. For example: 'I used this formula because I wanted first to reduce the number of variables'. In this method the problem-solving process is not interrupted as disturbingly as is the case with the questions and prompting method. The obvious disadvantage is that not all tasks involve dialogues (and changing the task may change the cognitive process) and that people will not verbalize all their thoughts in a dialogue situation.

2.6 Differences between methods

The methods described above differ on several dimensions with respect to validity (the report does not reflect the cognitive process) and completeness of the reports that they produce:

Invalid data due to disturbance of the cognitive process: The retrospection method will cause the least disturbance, the subject is not disturbed during the problem-solving itself. The only difficulty is that the solving process may change as a consequence of knowing that one is going to be asked questions afterwards. Questioning and prompting will give most disturbance. In the case of dialogues, the subject can partly do his or her own timing, but he or she may also be disturbed by the other person asking questions or making remarks. The disadvantage caused by disturbance in these cases lies not so much in the hampering of concentration, but in the possibility that thought processes take directions different from those they would have taken had the subject been left on his or her own.
Invalid and incomplete data due to memory errors: The data gathered, were they *post hoc* constructions or were they gathered on-line during the thought process? Prompting gives the most direct data. Retrospection of course only gives data after a time lapse. In the case of dialogues, people will sometimes directly give their arguments and questions, but sometimes they will wait a while. Memory errors can produce both incomplete and false reports.
Invalid and incomplete data due to interpretation by the subject: If the subject is asked to interpret his cognitive process or if he is required to do so by a structured technique that does not fit the content of the process this is a source of distortion and invalidity of the data with respect to the cognitive process. In the case of retrospection it is the subject who, for a large part, gives the initial interpretation of his or her behaviour.

The table below summarizes the techniques with respect to the method:

	Disturbance	Memory errors	Interpretation
Retrospection:	no	yes	yes
Introspection:	no	little	yes
Prompting:	yes	no	little
Dialogues:	not applicable	no	no
Structured techniques:	yes (?)	yes (?)	yes (?)

The question marks means that this is *generally* so.

In the case of structured techniques the risk of distorted data depends on details of the structuring and timing of the questions.

When one wants to study the thought processes themselves, and would like to know what is going on in a subject's mind from moment to moment, there is another method for obtaining verbal reports: asking the subject to think aloud during problem-solving.

2.7 Think aloud protocols

Thinking aloud is the method we will discuss in this book, so later on this method will be described extensively. To summarize: the subject is asked to talk aloud, while solving a problem and this request is repeated if necessary during the problem-solving process thus encouraging the subject to tell what he or she is thinking.

Thinking aloud during problem-solving means that the subject keeps on talking, speaks out loud whatever thoughts come to mind, while performing the task at hand. Unlike the other techniques for gathering verbal data, there are no interruptions or suggestive prompts or questions as the subject is encouraged to give a concurrent account of his thoughts and to avoid interpretation or explanation of what he is doing, he just has to concentrate on the task. This seems harder than it is. For most people speaking out loud their thoughts becomes a routine in a few minutes. Because almost all of the subject's conscious effort is aimed at solving the problem, there is no room left for reflecting on what he or she is doing. As discussed by Ericsson & Simon (1993), in general, talking out loud does not interfere with the task performance.

Thinking aloud is a method which, in principle, does not lead to much disturbance of the thought process. The subject solves a problem while the talking is executed almost automatically. The data so gathered are very direct, there is no delay. The subject does not give an interpretation of his or her thoughts nor is he or she required to bring them into a predefined form as in structured techniques. He or she renders them just as they come to mind. Think aloud protocols are not necessarily complete because a subject may verbalize only part of his thoughts. Compared with structured elicitation techniques, the think aloud method makes it easy for the subjects, because they are allowed to use their own language. Structuring the information is the task of the person who will analyse the protocols (see Chapter 7).

2.8 Combining methods

It is often possible to combine methods. The general principle is that one method is used to collect data that can be used to focus or facilitate application of the next method. We give a few examples:

Action protocol - retrospection: For some tasks retrospection can be supported by records of observations or intermediate products. For example, notes taken during problem-solving or a video of the problem-solving process can support the retrospection. This gives better results than just retrospection because the action protocol helps the subject to remember thoughts that he would not reconstruct otherwise.
Introspection - prompting: Introspection is used to identify critical events in a cognitive process, and in a second stage, subjects are prompted specifically about these events. This helps to overcome the effect of memory and interpretation by the subject and keeps the possibility to obtain more complete data about the process than would be possible by introspection alone.
Thinking aloud - retrospection: The think aloud protocols or behavioural observations during a session are used to obtain a retrospective protocol on pauses in the think aloud session or on fragments of the think aloud session that sounded incomprehensible, very incomplete or very odd. If possible this should be done directly after the think aloud session. If this is not feasible, one may show the written protocol to the subject and discuss the pauses, incomprehensible parts, etc. in a later stage.
Introspection - thinking aloud: Introspection is used to obtain a tentative model of the structure of the cognitive process. The think aloud method is then used to validate this model with more direct data. The result of introspection is used to help in the analysis of the protocols.

Literature

Maier's experiment is reported in Maier, 1931. The Ariadna system is described by Morgoev (1989). The extension that we sketched is inspired by the ASK system (Gruber, 1989). This article also contains an excellent discussion of the issues involved in building elicitation systems. Another discussion of such system with examples can be found in the collection by Marcus (1988). In Nisbett & Wilson, 1979, a number of studies are reviewed in which verbal reports could be shown to give false results. Ericsson & Simon (1993) showed that all these can be reduced to the factors that we discussed above: time delay and the effect of directed prompting. Their book contains a comprehensive review of the literature on the issues discussed in this book.

Chapter 3

The think aloud method

3.1 Introduction

In this chapter we discuss the history of the think aloud method and the conditions under which the method can be effectively used. Some of these conditions play an important role in knowledge acquisition and will be discussed separately. This chapter ends with an overview of the analysis process which will be discussed in the following chapters.

3.2 History of the think aloud method

The think aloud method has its roots in psychological research. It was developed from the older introspection method. Introspection is based on the idea that one can observe events that take place in consciousness, more or less as one can observe events in the outside world. Some early psychologists, for example Titchener (1929), went as far as to claim that the events in consciousness were the actual object of psychology in contrast to the outside world which is the object of the natural sciences. In this view, psychologists study the type of events that take place in human consciousness and their causal structure just as other scientists study the events that occur in the outside world. The analogy between introspection and observation was taken quite far. A methodological principle was for example, that only well trained observers (experienced psychologists) were to be used as observers because they would be able to interpret the events in consciousness in the right way, just as a biologist who observes animal behaviour may notice things that an ordinary observer will miss.

Introspection has led to some successful research but there were also fundamental theoretical and methodological problems attached to it. The theoretical problems concern the model of introspection as perception of the contents of consciousness. This model makes a separation between the processes in consciousness and the introspection process itself, thereby suggesting that the latter is not accessible in consciousness. If that were true, then how is the introspection process accessed by the observer? On the other hand, if both are considered to be accessible in consciousness, a 'homunculus' problem is raised: is the introspection process itself subject to introspection? These questions could not be answered satisfactorily within the framework of introspection as perception of consciousness. As we discussed in Chapter 2, the solution that underlies the think aloud method is to assume a simpler process (*verbalization* instead of observation and interpretation) and to assume that only the contents of working memory are verbalized instead of the entire cognitive process.

A methodological problem with more severe practical consequences is that in the introspection view the research data are the events that take place in consciousness. These are to be analysed and explained. However, these data are fundamentally accessible only to a single observer, who also performs the thought process. This makes it impossible to replicate empirical studies and thereby to settle scientific discussions about thought processes. These discussions and the built-in limitation of the introspection method made psychologists turn away from the introspectionist method and associated theories. Because introspection was a central method in studying cognitive processes, this also meant that psychological research turned away from cognitive processes. This contributed to the rise of behaviourism in the 1930s. Behaviourism took the other extreme view. It banned all theorizing about processes that cannot be observed from the outside of the body, as speculation, with the exception of physiological processes. (Physiology was considered a related field.) The history of the introspection method in psychology has made psychologists suspicious of methods that resemble introspection. Note that we know now that this suspicion is not justified with respect to the think aloud method for two reasons:

• The think aloud method avoids interpretation by the subject and only assumes a very simple verbalization process.
• The think aloud method treats the verbal protocols, that are accessible to anyone, as data thus creating an objective method.

There has been a 'thin' line of research even in the 1930s and 1940s that continued to experiment with variations of introspective methods. The main methodological advancement with respect to the introspective method was to treat the (verbal) reports as data, instead of the processes in consciousness. The advantage is that these data are open to inspection and interpretation for anyone. The theoretical model of the production of the verbal reports became less important, now that a working method became available. Interesting results were obtained with the think aloud method by for example Duncker (1945) and de Groot (1946 and 1965). Duncker analysed problem-solving processes in terms of memory search. He explained the sequence of possible solutions that people explore from an informal model of retrieval of relevant partial solutions from memory. These solutions were then accepted, modified or rejected by applying them to the problem and evaluating their implications. Without verbal data about the process this is clearly hard to investigate. De Groot was able to describe problem-solving by expert chess players as progressive refinement of a plan, using a large set of specific concepts and principles.

By the end of the 1960s the interest in internal cognitive processes grew very fast and thereby the interest in methods that can provide data about these processes. A major result was the work by Newell & Simon (1972), who used think aloud protocols in combination with computer models of problem-solving processes to build very detailed models. Using this methodology Newell and Simon were able to explain protocol data from a theory of human memory and assumptions about the knowledge that subjects could bring to bear on a task. This work had a major influence, because it showed that very detailed explanations of verbal data can be obtained. Although many psychologists were skeptical, the method gained more and more acceptance especially in the period from 1980 on, when computer simulations of cognitive processes became increasingly popular.

In the 1980s computer scientists began to develop expert systems. Using techniques from Artificial Intelligence, they demonstrated that it was possible to build programs that performed at an expert level of performance. Initially, however, there was no systematic way to obtain the knowledge from human experts. Knowledge engineers used more or less structured interviews with experts to obtain the initial version of a knowledge-base and in a later stage employed them as an oracle to repair errors in the program: a false solution that the program had found was shown to the expert, along with the trace of the solution process and the expert was asked to indicate where this had gone wrong and how the knowledge should be modified.

This method amounts to a combination of introspection and a structured form of prompting that suffers from the strengths and weaknesses of both: introspection is likely to miss many special tricks, heuristics, shortcuts and special case solutions and structured prompting is suggestive and imposes a particular format on the knowledge. In the worst case, this may focus the expert on an aspect of the problem that is actually not relevant and it may distort the knowledge (if the format is inadequate). Some of the expertise is built up by experience and cannot easily be articulated and explained to an outsider. This led some researchers to use the think aloud method to elicit expert knowledge. If the expert can apply his knowledge in problem-solving then this becomes visible in the protocols. In this way it became possible to obtain knowledge of which the expert was not aware and the free (verbal) format avoids distortions and misrepresentations.

Currently the think aloud method is accepted as a useful method by a large part of the scientific community in psychology and it also has its place in the repertoire of many knowledge engineers. In section 2.6 we discussed factors that threaten the validity and completeness of verbal data. These factors were: invalidity due to disturbance of the cognitive process, invalidity and incompleteness due to memory errors and invalidity and incompleteness due to interpretation by the subject. What is the position of the think aloud method with regard to these factors:

Invalidity due to disturbance of the cognitive process: Does the additional task of thinking aloud change the cognitive process? Will a different process take place than without thinking aloud? Consider the following example. A psychologist is interested in the way in which people operate a power plant. He instructs the operators to think aloud while they monitor and operate the control panel of the plant. However, at some point an operator seems to forget her instruction to think aloud and quickly takes a series of actions. If the think aloud instruction is repeated and emphasized then the operator becomes a bit irritated and begins to act differently. It seems that she now performs the task differently. Finally emotional and motivational factors can result in a cognitive process that is different from the process that would take place during task performance without thinking aloud. There is not much evidence that thinking aloud adds much to the effect of being studied and evaluated that is inevitable in knowledge acquisition and experimental settings. In the next chapter we discuss how to minimize these effects.

Invalidity and incompleteness due to memory errors: Errors due to incomplete or false recall are essentially absent in case of the think aloud method. In any case they are not comparable with the errors that are caused by reconstruction processes in memory.

Invalidity due to interpretation by the subject: In psychological experiments no evidence was found that think aloud protocols are inaccurate in the sense that people give incorrect information about the cognitive process concerned (other than occasional errors like those normally found in spoken language). This does not mean that protocols are easy to understand. As we already saw in Chapter 1, interpreting protocols can actually be quite difficult. As with other verbal reporting techniques, the form of the information and the verbal ability of the subject determine the quality of the reports. Sewing on a button or selecting spices for a sauce would not be easy to verbalize for most of us.

Although the think aloud method does not suffer from the threats to completeness and validity that play a role in the other techniques, it introduces two new threats to the validity of reports:

Incompleteness due to synchronization problems: Thinking aloud takes place concurrently with the cognitive process. A cognitive process takes longer when the think aloud method is used. This means that people are able to slow down the normal process to synchronize it with verbalization. However, subjects frequently report that sometimes verbalization does not keep up with the cognitive process and that their report is incomplete. This is consistent with the observation that occasionally protocols contain 'holes' of which it is almost necessary to assume that an intermediate thought occurred here.
Invalidity due to problems with working memory: If reasoning takes place in verbal form then verbalizing the contents of working memory is easy and uses no capacity of working memory. However, if the information is non-verbal and complicated then verbalization will not only cost time but also space in working memory because it becomes a cognitive process by itself. This will cause the report of the original process to be incomplete and it can sometimes even disrupt this process.

A related effect occurs when verbalizing the information in working memory is difficult and uses some of the capacity of working memory. For example, if the process operator wants to verbalize one of the items that quickly pass, she must keep it in memory while finding a suitable description of it. This memory space cannot be used for other information. This is a problem if she is used to quickly check several instruments and then consider the results. If she tries to follow her routine, then the capacity of working memory may be insufficient. Problems with working memory and synchronization can be recognized by complaints by the subject and interrupted verbalizations.

If you find that the think aloud method does not work well possibilities are to change the method, the task or the subjects. We have already discussed the range of applicable methods. Below we discuss the selection of subjects and tasks.

3.3 Selecting subjects

3.3.1 Criteria for selecting subjects

Both subjects and tasks must thus be selected that the effect of possible disruptive effects of thinking aloud is minimized. The cognitive process in which we are interested should occur when the task is presented to the subject, disruption of the process by thinking aloud should be minimized and so should synchronization problems and working memory overload. Both in scientific research and in knowledge acquisition one does not always have a choice. Research may be directed at a particular kind of persons and we need a random sample of those because the results must be generalized over all persons of this kind. In knowledge acquisition it is often difficult to get access to an expert and one often cannot choose. Two important properties of subjects with regard to the applicability of the think aloud method are the degree of expertise and verbalization skills.

3.3.2 Experts as subjects

If the think aloud method is used for the elicitation of expert knowledge several problems are likely to occur. Expert knowledge is often partially 'compiled' in the sense that experts are able to perform a task very well, but that they cannot explain how they found the right answer ('I just saw that it had to be this'). The think aloud method makes some of this knowledge visible. On several occasions we observed that experts were able to make their knowledge explicit in a discussion afterwards about their think aloud protocols and our analysis of the protocols. However, as with regular subjects, experts that perform a task as a routine and very fast, are unable to verbalize their thoughts during this performance.

One has to take into account social and motivational aspects in psychological research with human experts. These factors may induce a person to behave more rationally in a psychological laboratory than in a more natural setting. Being supervised by a psychologist may influence the reasoning processes in experts when they think aloud. Experts can be secretive about their expertise and they may be reluctant to give someone else insight in their actual problem-solving behaviour. Most experts are well aware that they cannot easily justify their answers (acting by their routine), but they may not want their audience to know this. Because of this, they may adopt a more rational reasoning style for the occasion of the knowledge acquisition session.

If you study expert behaviour with the goal of building a knowledge-based system, one could argue that the expert's rationalized problem-solving behaviour is not a problem, but a potential positive feature of a technique. Introspection or retrospection seem appropriate here because they yield more rational knowledge than the *ad hoc* reasoning that appears in practice. The target knowledge-based computer system should also be an optimal system rather than an imitation of the expert, including his weaknesses. However, in practice a 'rationalizing' expert may produce rationalizations that have no relation with the actual expertise and that are a much weaker basis for a knowledge-based system than the observed problem-solving behaviour. In particular, a rationalizing expert is likely to hide the unclear, poorly understood areas in his expertise, either in an effort to help the knowledge engineer by keeping things simple and avoiding the messy details, or by helping the knowledge engineer to find justifications for the answers. She may for example refuse to solve a problem because it has no justifiable solution even when she has a strong feeling about the best solution. It is better to use the think aloud sessions to acquire the expertise 'in action' and to find interpretations, explanations and generalizations quietly and systematically during analysis of the protocols. An expert should therefore be instructed that it is more important that the protocol is natural and direct than that it is comprehensible to the person taking the protocol (the knowledge engineer). Incomprehensible parts can always be cleared up afterwards, but missing thoughts and knowledge cannot be recovered. This means that one should take care to ensure the cooperativeness of the expert for the think aloud sessions. One way to achieve this, is by pointing out that this method may reveal patterns in his or her reasoning that are novel and by making clear that the expert will be involved in the analysis of the protocols.

3.3.3 Differences in verbalization skills

There are substantial differences in the ease with which people verbalize their thoughts. As we shall discuss in Chapter 4, a little training will help people to become more fluent, but differences remain, even after training. As a result some protocols will be more complete than others. If it is reasonable to assume that this skill is not associated with the cognitive process involved then one would of course prefer to select subjects with good verbalization skills. However, for most skills this is not known. In our experience, the quality of verbalizations is not strongly associated with other properties that can easily be observed or measured. One possible exception is age. Young children usually find it difficult to think aloud. It is not clear if this is due to their verbalization skills, to the content of their thought processes or to the general difficulty of concentrating on a problem-solving task. Here too, the only practical approach is to try out the think aloud procedure in a pilot session.

3.4 Selecting problems

The considerations that we listed for selecting subjects also apply to the selection of problems for use in think aloud sessions. We already mentioned that certain tasks are less suited because they involve non-verbal information or because speed is inherent in the task. Other factors may also interfere with the think aloud task. For example tasks that involve verbal communication (for example, air traffic control, psychotherapy) are in their original form not suited for the think aloud method. Also within a task area that is suitable (for example, solving physics problems or architectural design) it is not easy to select a task which gives good data. Important considerations are:

(a) Is the task at a level of difficulty that is appropriate for the subjects with respect to the cognitive process? The subjects should not be able to solve the problem in an automated manner. The task should be difficult enough.
(b) Is the task representative with respect to the cognitive process involved? One is sometimes tempted to select an unusual problem because only that will be difficult enough. A risk is then that it introduces matters that are only marginally relevant to the cognitive process one wants to study. A practical way to overcome this is asking the assistance of another expert in selecting several problems that are both difficult and not too far fetched. After the experimental session one should also ask the subjects if they felt that the problems were unusual in any sense.

Because of time restrictions it is usually possible to apply the think aloud method to only a rather small set of problems. The best way to handle this is probably to combine the think aloud method with less time-consuming techniques that make it possible to get a picture of the generality of the results that were obtained with the think aloud method.

3.5 Summary

Not all tasks or subjects are equally suited for the think aloud method. The purpose of the method is to obtain data about a cognitive process. Therefore the situation should be such that this target process takes place in 'optima forma' and that it is 'verbalizable' in the sense that it involves verbalizable contents on working memory, does not proceed too fast to allow synchronization and does not cause working memory overload. These factors are relative to subject and task. The same task may be automated or verbalizable for one person but not for another.

3.6 Overview of the analysis of think aloud protocols

After discussing the verbalization process and methodological aspects of collecting think aloud protocols, we shall now turn to the analysis of the protocols. Here we give an overview of the analysis process as it will be discussed in the following chapters. Figure 3.1 presents the objects that play a role in the analysis of think aloud protocols:

Psychological theory of problem-solving: This is a theory about one or more aspects of human problem-solving. Think aloud protocols are relevant for theories about aspects of problem-solving that appear during the problem-solving process (and not only factors that influence it or characteristics of problem-solving performance) and that are accessible to verbalization (see Chapter 5).
Task analysis: Normative and competence models of problem-solving, describing the best way to perform a task and possible alternatives. If a task is complicated and a detailed model is required (for example, a computer program that can perform a task) then a task analysis itself is constructed following intermediate steps. For example, one may first construct an informal sketch of the model, next a more detailed design and finally a computer program (see Chapters 5 and 6).
Psychological model: A task-specific model of the problem-solving process that is the result of applying the psychological theory to the task analysis. The result is a model that predicts from the psychological theory and from the structure of the task (and the knowledge required to perform it) how people will behave when performing the task. Just like the task analysis, the psychological model can also be built in steps, from an informal model to a computer simulation (see Chapters 5 and 6).

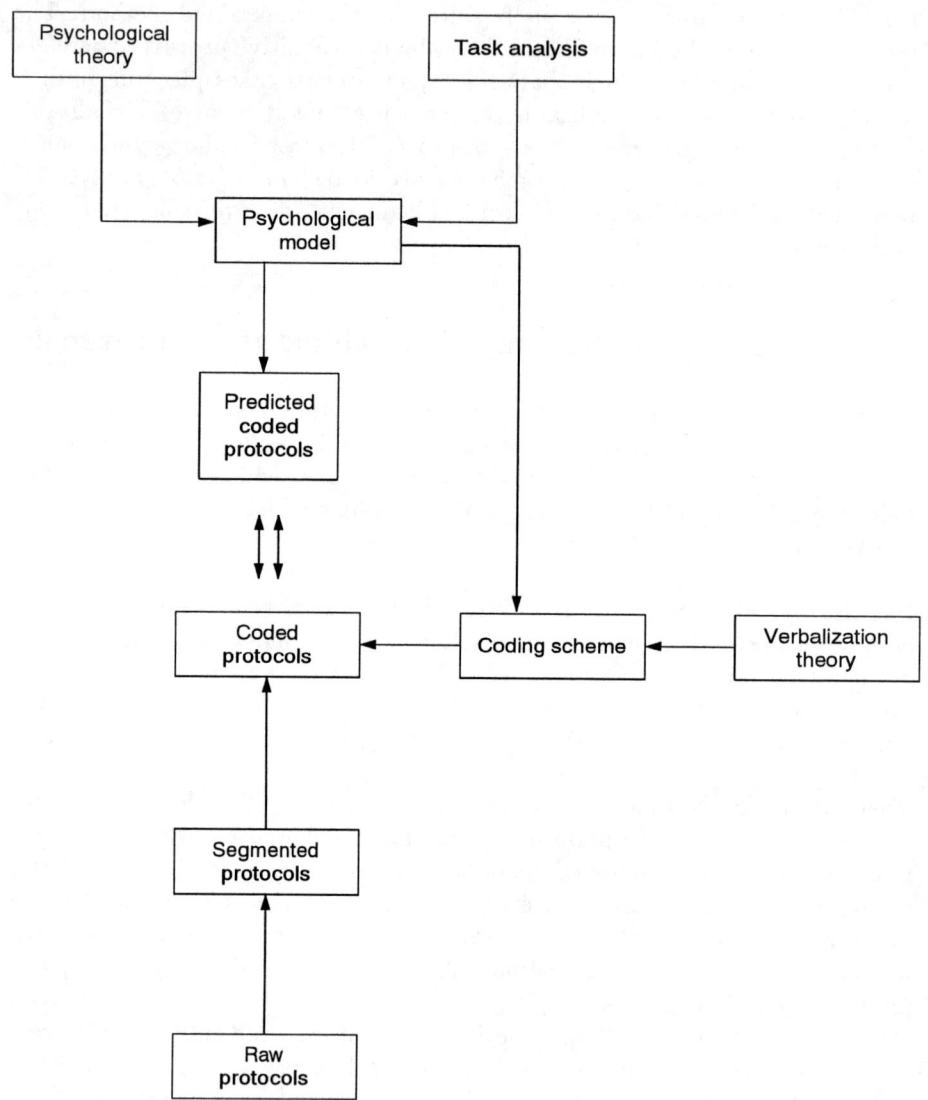

FIGURE 3.1: Overview of protocol analysis

Verbalization theory: This is a theory about the way in which thoughts that occur during problem-solving are verbalized. Verbalization itself is a task that has been studied in psychology and theories about cognitive processes can be applied here. This theory itself consists of a general psychological part (about the process of verbalization) and a part that is specific to the current task and the subject. Psychological theories about verbalization are usually not specific enough to construct a coding scheme and therefore it is necessary to use pilot protocols to obtain the vocabulary and phrasing that appear in protocols (see Chapter 7).
Coding scheme: An operationalization of the psychological model, that relates the psychological model to the text of the think aloud protocols. It is in the form of a coding scheme for protocol fragments. The coding scheme is obtained by applying verbalization theory to the psychological model (see Chapter 7).
Coded protocols: By applying the coding scheme to the protocols, coded protocols can be obtained.
Predicted coded protocols: The psychological model should imply predictions for the coded protocols (see Chapter 7).
Segmented protocols: The first step in the analysis is to divide the protocols into segments (see Chapter 7).
Raw protocols: This refers to protocols that are transcribed from the audio recording, possibly extended with other data such as notes or observations (see Chapter 4).

Literature

Pioneers of the use of the think aloud method in knowledge acquisition were Breuker & Wielinga (1987). The best source on the history and validity of the think aloud method is Ericsson & Simon, 1993. This gives an extensive discussion of the psychological literature on the method.

Chapter 4

Practical procedures in obtaining think aloud protocols

4.1 Introduction

It is not difficult to collect think aloud protocols, but small errors in the procedure can render the data almost useless. In this chapter we describe the practical procedures to be applied in experiments where subjects are asked to think aloud. Most of the procedures for obtaining think aloud protocols apply to both applications for psychological research and for knowledge acquisition. We use the terms *subject* and *experimenter* for both situations. In terms of the overview of protocol analysis we gave at the end of Chapter 3, this chapter deals with the obtaining of raw protocols.

4.2 Setting

The first thing to do when one wants to get a subject to think aloud is to make sure that the setting is such that the subject feels at ease. The subject should be settled comfortably. The room should be quiet, a glass of water should be at hand, the chair should be comfortable. Although this holds for all kinds of psychological research, it is especially important to remember in the case of thinking aloud, particularly when an experiment is going to take quite some time and will be tiresome for the voice and throat of the subject.

The situation should be focused on the task and the experimenter should interfere as little as possible with the thought process to avoid influencing its course.

In the case of a psychological study, an explanation can be given about the purpose of the research, about what is going to happen and about the protection of the data. It may be wise to emphasize that you are interested in the way people solve problems, and not in unconscious emotions and hidden thoughts. People may have reservations about this kind of research and it is best that you make your purpose clear and explain that there are no hidden motives. Explaining that the data are to be handled strictly confidentially is important. Not only is privacy protection a matter of ethics and of legal practice, it is also important for the research itself. When the subject is very nervous, this may hinder his speaking out loud. This is not a negligible factor. When asking people to talk while they are performing a task, you ask them to bring out into the open the way they tackle a problem. This may be very embarrassing. For example, the physics student may be used to solve problems by randomly trying some formulas. Yet she may be quite well aware of the fact that there is a neat, consistent way of solving the problem. She may not like to give the impression that she just messes around. And when a task is supposed to be quite easy for an expert, the same expert may feel discomfort at having to admit that he does not find it easy at all. Or the expert may be inclined to simplify the problem-solving process for the alleged benefit of the experimenter.

In the context of knowledge acquisition it is important to make the experts collaborate. Otherwise the validity of the data is threatened: the expert may behave differently from his normal way of performing the task and avoid reasoning steps of which he himself is not certain. An acknowledged expert in a certain domain, for example, would not like to run the risk of his boss knowing about his failing to solve certain problems. And unnecessary anxiety may hamper the whole experimental procedure. Thus to create an atmosphere of confidence and easiness is of the utmost importance.

4.3 Instructions

Instructions about the task at hand should be given as customary. The instruction on thinking aloud is quite simple. The essence of the instruction is: Perform the task and say out loud what comes to your mind. Write down the instructions beforehand and read them to the subject. Here are some examples of instructions:

'I will give you a problem. Please keep talking out loud while solving the problem.'

'Please solve the following problems and while you do so, try to say everything that goes through your mind.'

Part of the instruction used by Hamel (1990) in his study on architectural design was as follows:

You will in a moment receive a design task. You are asked to perform this task in the way you are used to go about a commission in your daily practice. It is important that you say aloud everything that you think or do in designing.

It is better not to use phrases like: 'Tell me what you think'. People may think that you are asking for their opinion, or for an evaluation of their thoughts. This instruction would also suggest that a problem must be solved by real thinking and they would not feel free to report ideas that just occurred to them, apparently not as part of a rational goal-directed thought process. Do not make the instruction too long. The more you say, the more subjects will make up their own interpretations about what it is you want from them.

4.4 Warming up

Although most people do not have much difficulty rendering their thoughts, there are some subjects for whom this method does not work. Most subjects need a little training but after some time, usually a few minutes to a quarter of an hour, most subjects will talk quite automatically. When after a quarter of an hour a subject still finds it hard to verbalize his thoughts, it is better to stop because this subject is unlikely to provide useful protocols.

Give the subject an opportunity to practice thinking aloud. Sometimes the task they have to perform will also ask for a practice phase. Then it is efficient to use that phase to practice thinking aloud as well. If the task does not involve such phase, one has to look for a task to practice on. In general it is wise to look for a task which is not too different from the target task. An example of a practice task is:

A bottle of wine costs £5. The wine costs £4.50 more than the bottle. How much does the bottle cost?

In Appendix B, some examples of tasks are given. Some of the easy versions of those tasks may be used as practice tasks. The think aloud instruction for the practice task is the same as for the main task. Practising does not only give the subject an opportunity to familiarize himself with thinking aloud, but it also gives the experimenter an opportunity to train the subject to stick to verbalizing his thoughts and not to interpret the thoughts. If the subject offers interpretations and starts analysing his or her own problem-solving processes, the experimenter has to correct the subject and explain anew what the subject is supposed to do and not to do. One should not start with the real session before one is confident that the subject is feeling comfortable with the task of thinking aloud. It is better to prolong the practising phase than to have to interfere in the target task or to end up with a useless protocol.

4.5 Behaviour of the experimenter and prompting

When the subject is working on the task, the role of the experimenter is a restrained one. Interference should only occur when the subject stops talking. Then the experimenter should prompt the subject by just, and only just saying: 'Keep on talking'. This is usually enough to keep the subject engaged in thinking aloud for some time. It is a hard job for the experimenter. Especially when the experimenter is familiar with the task domain, he is inclined to correct the subject when going wrong or help the subject along when stuck. This really must be avoided. So the experimenter should have some experience in gathering think aloud data, in particular in avoiding unnecessary interference.

4.6 Recording

The session is usually recorded on audio- or video-tape. It may be wise to include the instruction and the practising phase, in order to be able to check afterward whether the procedure was performed correctly. It may sound rather trivial, but always check and double check the recording instruments; you would not be the first to end up with an empty tape after a long session with a unique subject. Also check your equipment regularly during the session, as inconspicuously as you can.

4.7 Transcription of the protocol

After the session has been recorded, it has to be transcribed. Typing out complete protocols is usually inevitable in psychology to be able to apply reliable coding procedures. In knowledge engineering it is always useful to transcribe an initial set of protocols, but later on protocols can be transcribed more selectively: only parts that show new knowledge or new reasoning processes need to be transcribed.

Transcribing a protocol usually means typing it out as verbatim as possible. This typing out brings along its own difficulties. Typing out protocols is a tedious and time-consuming task. Transcribing may take about 10 times as much time as the original protocol, depending on the clarity of the protocol and the fluency of the subject. People may have accents which are strange to the typist, they may mumble, they may have a habit of not completing their words, etc. Still, even if the subject talks very clearly, there will be many instances where it is difficult to understand what exactly the subject is saying. The subject may interrupt himself in the middle of a word, he may whisper something, he may make strange noises. It is also possible that during the session a noise was made in or outside the room that obscures the voice of the subject. Sometimes it may help when the typist asks another person to try to hear what the subject said. However, it is sometimes impossible to understand what exactly was said. Instances like these should be marked in the typed out protocol, for example by typing 'unintelligible'.

This leads us to another important problem: what should be noted down and what can be left out? In psychological research, in principle everything can be relevant and therefore basically everything should be typed out. That is to say everything that was said during the session: the thinking out loud of the subject and the instructions and interruptions by the experimenter, including also utterances by the subject which have no bearing on the problem-solving process at all. For example, asking for a glass of water, or a remark about the rain which suddenly started. Sometimes the session was interrupted. Someone came into the room, asking for something, an announcement was made on the building's intercom. All these things should be noted down, identifying the speaker. It is important to know what happened during a session, because interruptions may have an influence on the problem-solving process. It is also a check on whether the experimenter behaved correctly and refrained from helping the subject a little. Off-side remarks by the subject may also be an indication of an impasse in the thought process. Getting stuck plays an important role in most problem-solving theories. When do people get into impasses and how do they resolve them? Noticing impasses may be of importance for further analysis of the protocol. A difficult problem is how to type out a subject's 'humming and hawing'. Most people say things like 'Er, I er ...'. Generally speaking, the typist should try to type it out as faithfully as he can, staying as close as possible to what the subject said. This is sometimes hard and leads to rather ugly protocols. Stammering as well should be typed out just as it occurred.

Recognizable pauses and unusual silences between two words are noted down by special marks, conventionally by dots, for example: 'I guess ... the answer is ten'. A long silence may be transcribed as 'silence'. Some transcribers give more dots for a longer silence. However, when should a pause be considered unusual? And when is it long? It is a matter of interpretation by the typist. But on the other hand, the human ear is well trained for detecting unusual pauses between words in a sentence.

Punctuation is another point to consider. When a complete and grammatically correct sentence is spoken, it is easy to type a full stop or a comma. However, most sentences in think aloud protocols are not so well-formed. One should therefore be careful with punctuation, in order not to give one's own interpretation to a sentence. It is often wise not to use punctuation at all, and to start a new line for each new sentence - or when one thinks a new sentence starts. Especially question marks should be avoided, as it is often hard to be sure whether some utterance was meant as a question or as a positive remark.

Still, how should one go about the intonation of the subject? Sometimes one can hear perfectly well that the subject said something questioningly. Or angrily, depressedly, cheerfully. Some researchers note down the intonation of the subject as such. However, research shows that the reliability of observations of this kind is very low, and that people hear different things when listening to the same tape.

When a protocol has been recorded on video or other data such as notes or observations are available, it is convenient to insert the action protocol into the protocol, usually in a separate column next to the protocol text. For example: 'the subject takes up his pencil', 'the subjects looks in the book'. The same goes for data noted down by the experimenter, or recorded by a log file on the computer, for example 'the subject types in 43 + 21'. Notes concerning these data should be clearly distinguished from the think aloud protocol. The question here is, what do we do with observations which are not clearly objective? For example: 'the subjects seems to bite his pencil and tries to think hard', 'the subject looks around'. If one wants to make this kind of observations, because they might be useful later on, the best thing to do is to note them down separately from the other data.

All of the problems sketched above have to do with one central theme: avoiding unwarranted interpretation. One wants to analyse and to model the protocols, so one needs transcriptions which differ as little as possible from the real protocols as recorded on tape. Later on the subject's behaviour has to be interpreted in the light of the model one uses for analysing the protocols. So, what is needed are transcriptions of protocols in which interpretation does not play a (large) role. Although it is impossible to avoid interpretation altogether, one has to try to keep it out of the transcription. Protecting measures which can be taken are the following. Let someone else than the experimenter type out the protocols. Give the typist very careful instructions to transcribe the protocol as literal as possible and to avoid any restructuring, improvements to the style and grammar and avoiding interpretations. If something is unclear on the audio-tape then it better to type 'unclear' than to interpret it at that stage. One could even let another person compare the transcription to the tape. Although these are sound measures, they are often not feasible. Typing out protocols takes a large amount of time and there may be no one else available but the experimenter. For example, when subjects use a lot of specialized jargon, it may be nearly impossible for a secretary to type out the protocol.

Sometimes it is not necessary to type out the complete protocol. It may be more efficient to encode protocols directly from the tape. Especially if a very coarse grained coding system is used or if you are only interested in some specific actions in the protocols. For example: if you want to know what information sources a problem solver uses, such as books or a teacher, you are only interested in those sections of the protocol where a reference is made to an information source. In this case it is possible just to listen to the tape and note down a code every time an information source is mentioned.

Although direct encoding from audio-tape instead of transcribing and coding the transcription seems attractive in terms of efficiency, it is often not a method to be recommended. There are several reasons:

(a) In many cases the data may be subject to several cycles of interpretation, each time with a revised coding scheme. This can be done much more efficient with written protocols. Especially in an exploratory phase of a project, protocols are used for model building and this is of course much easier from a written down protocol.
(b) Objectivity: it is difficult for another researcher to inspect whether your coding is correctly performed.
(c) The context effect: it is not possible in this procedure to avoid the effect of the context on coding protocol fragments (see also Chapter 7).

The best procedure is to use direct encoding only in a late stage of the research, when the model and the coding scheme are fixed. In the near future computer technology may make it easier to analyse verbal recordings without transcribing them, see Section 7.8.

4.8 Review

Reviewing the protocol with the subject can provide very useful additional information. Protocols are usually incomplete and difficult to interpret and the subject can be very helpful here. A good procedure is to review the protocol with the subject as soon as possible after the actual think aloud session. In psychological research the additional comments and explanations that are given during the review should not be treated in the same manner as the protocol, because they have a different status (retrospective instead of think aloud data).

Chapter 5

Building models of problem-solving

5.1 Introduction

Now that we have discussed how to obtain and document think aloud protocols, we turn to analysis of these protocols. The purpose of the collection and analysis of protocols is the study of cognitive processes. This means that we want to construct or test a process model. In this chapter we will first discuss the purpose of constructing models. Next we explain how the process of building models can be divided into analysing the task and applying psychological theory. We will discuss in detail how such models can be constructed. The psychological model forms the core of the protocol analysis. We will give several detailed examples in order to familiarize the reader with concepts and procedures in protocol analysis.

5.2 Modelling cognitive processes

In knowledge engineering the purpose of the analysis is to construct a computer system that embodies part of the knowledge and skills of a human expert. One may think that the reasoning process of a human expert is not really relevant for building intelligent computer systems. The main point in that view is that the system should just give correct solutions to problems irrespective of how the human expert solves those problems. However, as we mentioned in Chapter 1, the reasoning process of the expert is relevant to building knowledge-based systems for several reasons:

Explanation: Many knowledge-based computer systems are required to 'explain' their solutions. To be understandable for human users of these systems, these explanations best show correspondence to the knowledge used in an expert's problem solving process. The reasoning steps can be incorporated in the computer system to enable the system to explain its solution to a problem.
Breaking down knowledge acquisition: It is usually not possible to present all possible problems to an expert and ask her to find a solution for each of them. Breaking the task down into reasoning steps and modelling each step makes it possible to avoid this. Consider a medical diagnosis task that we shall discuss more elaborately in Chapter 8. The givens for a diagnostic problem, data about a patient, consist of answers to some 40 questions. There are about 15 possible diagnoses. This gives a very large number of possible problems (i.e. possible descriptions of patients). It is of course impossible to present all possible patient descriptions to an expert and ask him or her for a diagnosis. However, several groups of properties are associated with underlying properties. For example, several different descriptions of pain actually refer to a particular type of pain: 'cardiac pain'. This can be exploited by separately acquiring knowledge about recognizing 'cardiac pain' and then finding out how 'cardiac pain' is related to the possible diagnoses. This structuring of the task reduces the amount of knowledge that has to be acquired from the expert. This makes it so important to find the expert's reasoning steps.
Validation: A related point is validation of the knowledge in a computer system by an expert. It is often necessary to have the knowledge in the final system validated by an expert. As in acquisition, the decomposition that can be achieved by validating reasoning is that the system gives the correct solutions to problems.

All this means that in knowledge acquisition the reasoning process of the expert must be modelled and not only the relation between the givens and solutions of problems. In psychology the interest for cognitive processes is a matter of taste and paradigm. Some researchers are not interested in processes but only in overall relations between properties of people, situations and visible behaviour but others believe that fairly detailed understanding of cognitive processes is the key to understanding human behaviour. Protocol analysis is only useful if one is interested in these processes. In this chapter we discuss the construction of models of cognitive processes.

5.3 The form of models of cognitive processes

Descriptions of cognitive processes can take different forms. The most important forms are *dimensional models, categorical models* and *procedural models*. A dimensional model means that a protocol is rated on one or more dimensions. These dimensions concern the cognitive process. For example, we can define properties such as 'duration', 'number of reasoning steps' or 'extent to which the problem data are used' and find a way to measure these. The model predicts ratings for different types of people or tasks. A categorical model assigns categories of cognitive processes to a protocol. An example is 'checks applicability of formula before using it'. Of course not all dimensions of cognitive processes require think aloud protocols. Solution times can simply be measured and other dimensions or categories can be measured from the product or from visible behaviour.

A model of cognitive processes can be defined in terms of properties of the processes (either as dimensions or as categories) but a different way is to construct a model in the form of *procedures*. A procedural model describes a sequence of steps. Consider again the protocol of word problems given in Chapter 1. A procedure that describes at least part of this protocol is the following:

Procedure Algebraic(in: text; out: solution):
1. Read the problem text(text; sentences)
2. Translate each sentence into an algebraic equation (sentences; equations)
3. Solve the resulting set of equations for the unknown (equations; solution)

This very simple model describes step by step the cognitive process that takes place during problem-solving. In this case the procedural model simply consists of a sequence of steps that are described in very abstract terms. However, each of these steps could be elaborated in more detail, including the information that they use and produce. For example, the step 'translate each sentence into an algebraic equation' can be elaborated by specifying the possible sentences appearing in the arithmetic word problems (the information used), possible algebraic equations (possible results of the translation step) and the steps that are needed to perform the translation. In that case we would construct a general procedural model that can be applied to a wide range of problems and that describes different solution traces depending on the problem to which it is applied. For example, a procedural model for solving arithmetic word problems could contain a sub-procedure as follows:

Procedure Translate(in: sentence; out: equation):
FOR EACH sentence:
IF sentence = 'A has N Z' THEN equation = 'A = N1'
IF sentence = 'B has N Z more than C' THEN equation = 'N = B - C'
etc.

This procedure would translate sentences like *Mary has 5 apples* into: 'Mary = 5'. This procedure will of course produce different results depending on the data. For each problem it can generate a *solution trace*. This trace can be viewed as a prediction for the cognitive process as it appears in the protocol. It is obvious that fully specifying such procedures will be a complicated exercise. The amount of detail that is needed depends on the need for a computational model and on the amount of detail that is relevant for the original research question about the cognitive process.

Once a procedure is specified, it can be used in two directions: (1) to *generate* a reasoning process (or a description of it) or (2) to *recognize* a given process. For example, we can compare a given sequence of reasoning steps with a procedure to see if this process *can* be generated by the procedure. If this is the case, the sequence of reasoning steps *satisfies* the procedure. Consider the example above. Suppose that we observe that a person reads the sentence: *Mary has 5 apples* and says: `'OK, Mary 5'` This suggests that he applied the procedure 'Translate', as described above because the result of the procedures is the same as the verbalization.

The procedural model above is similar to a computer program in the sense that both generate reasoning steps when they are applied to a problem. The main difference between the procedure above and a computer program is that a computer program is written in a programming language, a language that can be executed by a computer system. A model that is written in an executable programming language is called a computational model.

In knowledge acquisition the ultimate goal of protocol analysis is to construct a computer program based on the knowledge that becomes visible in the protocols. In psychology, it can be useful to construct a computer program that generates behaviour that can be compared to the protocols. However, for many analyses informally specified procedures are adequate. We shall discuss languages for procedural models, including programming languages in detail in the next chapter. In this chapter we focus on the problem of dealing with the complexity, the richness and the initial obscurity of think aloud protocols.

5.4 Procedural models and explanation of human behaviour

In knowledge acquisition it is obviously the ultimate goal to construct a full computational model for a task. In psychological or educational research the status of procedural models and the need for them is subject to discussion and debate. In this book we present the analysis of think aloud protocols as a method for data analysis. The protocols are data and the goal is to construct a psychological model that describes the data. The main differences between this method and other research methods in psychology are the unstructured verbal data and the use of procedural models. A question that is often raised concerns the meaning of the procedural model. A procedural model will contain elements (sub-procedures, production rules, etc.) that can be interpreted as descriptions of components of the human mind. Our position in this book is the following:

(a) It is not always necessary to make claims about the meaning of each aspect of a model. Consider componential models of intelligence that are formulated as numerical functions of performance measures or studies of cognitive skills that have the form of linear models of reaction times. Not all elements in such a mathematical expression can be interpreted in terms of cognitive processes or cognitive structures.

(b) It is attractive to hypothesize that components of a procedural model correspond directly to components of the mind but this requires additional evidence. There are many different procedural models that can account for protocols and additional psychological constraints are needed to select the correct one.

This brief discussion also clarifies in which sense procedural models 'explain' cognitive behaviour. A psychological model explicitly relates properties of the task and hypotheses about human problem-solving to (verbal) behaviour. When designing the model one is often forced (or at least tempted) to introduce elements that are needed to complete a model. These may be new discoveries about the task or new psychological hypotheses and in this sense they have a special status in the model.

5.5 Building models

In Chapter 3 the entire process of protocol analysis is summarized in Figure 3.1. In this chapter we are concerned with the upper part of this diagram, presented in Figure 5.1.

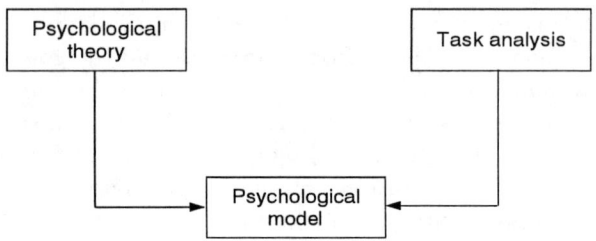

FIGURE 5.1: Constructing a psychological model

The principle that underlies the analysis is that the content of the protocols can be predicted from from the structure of the task, psychological knowledge and knowledge about the verbalization process (see Chapter 7 for the latter). *Task analysis* and *psychological theory* are used to construct a *psychological model* of the problem-solving process. We will discuss these three issues in greater detail.

The last example protocol in Section 1.1 exemplifies these phenomena. This protocol comes from a collection of protocols of 30 arithmetic word problems solved by over 40 subjects. This resulted in a large number of pages of protocols of which half a page is reproduced in Chapter 1. Although some of these protocols are less obscure than the one shown here, one can imagine the feelings of the psychologist who collected these protocols with a general interest in the way in which children solve these problems and why they find them so hard. The first impression is discouraging, to say the least. This experience is equally common in the use of think aloud protocols of experts. Expert protocols are often equally obscure. There are several principles to help dealing with this complexity:

Abstraction: Especially computational procedural models require very much detail. This leads to very complex models. One method to deal with this complexity is to define layers of abstraction. As we shall discuss in the next chapter languages for procedural models allow the definition of layers of abstraction. For example, a complex process can be defined as a top-level process and sub-processes. Abstraction should focus on aspects of the protocols that

are relevant for a particular problem. A psychologist may for example be interested in different aspects of the problem-solving process than a knowledge engineer. Psychologists can also be interested in different aspects of problem-solving processes. For example, one may be interested in the cause of errors, the effect of education, individual differences in cognitive styles, cognitive skills or general intelligence. Such different interests will result in different models and analyses. The interest must focus the analysis and the process must be modelled from the viewpoint of this interest. Starting with no initial viewpoint or interest is of course difficult. This will lead to gradual development of a viewpoint and corresponding abstractions but that tends to take much effort. The level of detail to which a model must be elaborated depends on the level of detail required for coding the protocols later on. A coarse-grained model is usually more difficult to compare with protocols than a detailed model. If a computational model is required then this will determine the level of detail.
Separate task analysis and psychological theory: In case of psychological research it is usually necessary to construct a model that explicitly states the meaning of the psychological theory *in the context of the task* and that provides more detail on the process than is implied by the psychological theory. Usually there are many other sources available to construct a first approximation of the cognitive behaviour by only looking at possible ways to perform the task. Examples of these sources are textbooks, interviews, etc. Using this information to build a first approximation of a model is called *task analysis*.

5.6 Task analysis

5.6.1 The construction of a task analysis

The structure of a procedural model is based on the idea that cognitive processes can be explained from three factors:

The problem: The information given as problem data and the question that together form the problem obviously have an effect on the problem-solving behaviour. Given the same knowledge and the same mechanism for applying it, different problems will result in different problem-solving behaviours.
The knowledge available to the problem solver: The knowledge about the task, consisting of facts, rules, principles, methods, strategies and the like clearly has an effect on problem-solving. This is immediately obvious, for example, from the example protocols given in Chapter 1.
The cognitive architecture: The cognitive architecture is the mechanism

for applying the knowledge. Properties of this mechanism have an effect on the behaviour. As we shall discuss later in this chapter, an important explanatory concept is the capacity limit of human working memory. This is part of the machinery that applies knowledge and has an effect on the way in which problems are solved.

Task analysis means constructing a first approximation of the model from information about the task without taking specific psychological factors into account. These will be 'added' in the next step. For many tasks there are sources that are more accessible than think aloud protocols and it is a good idea to exploit these first before trying the more complex protocol data. One useful source are *existing models* that have been constructed for similar tasks. The literature on Artificial Intelligence, knowledge-based systems and cognitive science contains a wide variety of methods, strategies, models and reasoning mechanisms that can be used as the basis of procedural models of problem-solving. Another important source are *textbooks and manuals* about particular tasks such as architectural design, solving physics problems and solving arithmetic word problems. Textbooks and manuals present the basic concepts and methods for a task. This information is often complementary to the computational models because these models emphasize the methods and the process structure instead of the knowledge that is specific to a task. Our experience is that textbooks are not nearly sufficient to construct a model of the problem-solving process. For example, textbooks tend to leave out knowledge that is essential to solve problems. However, they usually do a good job at providing an outline of the procedure and a set of important concepts. Most textbooks do not take into account psychological aspects of problem-solving. For example, they do not tell you how to avoid forgetting relevant information, how to organize the problem-solving process efficiently, etc. They tend to focus on the knowledge that is to be used. Therefore, even if it is possible to construct a more or less accurate procedure for solving problems, this is unlikely to be an accurate description of the way in which people actually solve problems.

Although in general other sources are used for the task analysis, one can also use *very clear and comprehensible* think aloud protocols at this stage. This use of protocols is called 'bottom-up'. Bottom-up use of protocols means finding abstract descriptions for parts of protocols. By recognizing similarities between different parts, abstractions can be defined that are assembled into a procedural model (or a property-based model). The top-down strategy needs an initial model to start from. This model is sometimes obtained from an initial holistic impression of a set of protocols but it can very well be based on other sources such as introspective reports, prescriptive methods, etc. This model is used to categorize parts of the protocol. If necessary, the model is extended or refined. (In the context of empirical research it is important, though, to separate the stages of exploratory research aimed at finding a theory or a model and of testing a hypothesis. As we shall discuss in Chapter 7 one should not use the same dataset for both stages.)

The risk of the bottom-up approach is that it is not possible to find good categories by inspecting only part of the data. In that case one ends up in the following cycle: an idea comes up when reading a protocol fragment. This is noted down. The context forces qualification of this idea, which gives a revised version. Next the idea is applied to other protocols, where it may reappear in a somewhat different form - or not at all. At some point the analysis will have to get a focus: a focus on a sub-process, a selection of important properties of a cognitive process or a model of the process that abstracts from certain details. Our advice is therefore to avoid the pure bottom-up approach.

The risk of the top-down strategy is that the initial model (or one of its refinements) is not adequate for the data. Because this model determines the rest of the analysis, this leads to complicated model revisions or to models that have a poor fit with the data. This analysis suggests that it is better to avoid both extremes and follow a mixed strategy: start from the safe side. If a highly plausible model can be obtained from sources that are more accessible and yet appropriate then start from there. If the interpretations of the data are very clear, start from there. This gives a mixed strategy.

Finally, a good method for task analysis that is easy to apply is simply *introspection*. Solving the task and reflecting on your own thoughts is a very sensible and respectable technique for task analysis.

5.6.2 Example: task analysis of solving arithmetic word problems

Suppose that we want to know how children solve arithmetic word problems and why they have difficulty with certain types of problems. First consider the problem data. In Chapter 1 we gave a few examples of arithmetic word problems:

Problem 1: *A father, a mother and their son are 80 years old together. The father is twice as old as the son. The father has the same age as the mother. How old is the son?*

Problem 2: *Irene has 6 sweets less than Suzanne. Diana has 5 more than Suzanne. How many sweets does Irene have less than Diana?*

These are two examples of a wide range of problems that together form the task *arithmetic word problems*. What they have in common is that they give information about quantities in the form of ordinary sentences. A problem may involve two or more numbers. The information may concern quantities or relations between quantities. In general arithmetic word problems do not require scientific knowledge (such as physics) but only common sense knowledge.

Suppose that we are interested in understanding the way in which children solve such problems, for example, to understand differences in level of difficulty between types of problems, the errors that children make and the knowledge that is needed to solve them, for example for teaching purposes. One may expect that the direct approach is the best: collect think aloud protocols and try to understand what is happening. Consider again the protocols in Chapter 1. The protocols about the first problem are relatively clear and one can construct a procedural model from them. The last example protocol shows that this is not always feasible. It is better to first analyse the task using other sources than the protocols and then return to the protocol. We use the task analysis to find an initial approximation of the knowledge needed to perform this task.

The algebraic method
How can arithmetic word problems be solved? One method that is taught in secondary school is the *algebraic method*. We summarized this method before in section 5.3. The problem is translated into algebraic equations and these are solved by standard algebraic procedures. If we apply this method to Problem 1 we get:

1. Note that the quantities are associated with the ages of *father*, *mother* and *son*. These become the variables in the equations.
2. Translating the sentences of Problem 1 gives the following equations:
age-father + age-mother + age-son = 80
age-father = 2 × age-son
age-mother = age-father
3. These equations can be solved for 'age-son' in various ways that we shall not describe here. The result represents the age of the son and is therefore the solution to the problem.

What is the knowledge required for this task? From Problem 1 it may seem that translating sentences into equations is a relatively straightforward process that requires little knowledge. The knowledge seems to be in the style of the procedure Translate in section 5.3 and so simple that it is not likely to cause errors. However, consider the following problem:

Problem 3: *A bottle of wine costs £5. The wine costs £4.50 more than the bottle. How much does the bottle cost?*

The second and third sentence suggest that quantities are associated with the wine, the bottle and the bottle of wine. This would give the following equations:

price-wine = 4.50
price-bottle-of-wine = 5

Now the 'price-bottle' is asked. However, this set of equations cannot be solved for 'price-bottle'! It requires some interpretation to see that 'price-bottle of wine' does not refer to a third object with an associated quantity but to the sum of 'price-wine' and 'price-bottle'. This initial analysis shows that there are at least two sub-processes: translate the sentences in the problem into algebraic equations and solve the equations for the asked.

The approximation method
The second method to solve arithmetic word problems is the *approximation method*. This is not taught in schools but it is known as a method for solving mathematical equations and also as a form of means-ends analysis, a more general problem-solving method defined in Artificial Intelligence. The sentences in the problem are viewed as *constraints* on unknown values that appear in the problem. Possible values for these must satisfy these *constraints*. This means that the sentences must be true or at least possibly true after filling in the possible answer.

Procedure Approximate:
1. Note the objects and their possible values.
As in the previous method these are:

price-of-bottle
price-of-wine
price-bottle-and-wine
price-bottle minus price-wine

The latter two are known. The first two can be (almost) anything. However, if we have a value for the price of the bottle or of the wine, the given values can be used to compute the missing one.
2. Generate a candidate solution for the asked quantity. In the current problem we would generate the candidate 'price of bottle = 50p'.
3. Substitute the solution into the problem text. In the example this would give: *A bottle of wine costs £5. The wine costs £4.50 more than the bottle. The bottle costs 50p.*
4. If this gives a consistent story then the candidate is the solution, else an inconsistency occurs. In the latter case, use the inconsistency that occurs in the story to decide if the candidate solution is too big or too small and use this feedback to generate a new candidate.

This would imply that the wine costs £5 and the bottle with the wine £5.50, which in turn is inconsistent with the first sentence in the story. Now we must decide if the candidate value for the bottle is too big or too small. Since the inconsistency was caused by a sum of bottle and wine that was too big, it is likely that the value of 50p. for the bottle was too high. The pure approximation method now reduces the value by an arbitrary amount, continuing this procedure until the right answer has been found.

This method is clearly more useful if only specific outcomes are allowed, for example only integer values. If real numbers are allowed the approximation process will not automatically halt and a criterion for stopping the approximation process is required. Each step in the approximation method requires knowledge: verifying a candidate solution, deciding if the candidate is too small or too large, estimating the size of the discrepancy. Again this is no trivial knowledge. We shall not elaborate this here but leave it as an exercise to the reader. Also note that some knowledge appears in all procedures.

The schema application method
A third method is taken from the psychological literature. It is based on the notion of *schema*: a structured abstract description. This *schema application* method identifies a schema in memory that fits the description in the story. Associated with this schema are procedures or other schemata with which the asked can be found. The literature is less clear about the details of these schemata and about how they are retrieved. One type of schemata that has been proposed refers to the states and events in the problem text in terms of the following classification:

Combine events: The text describes quantities that are somehow put to-

gether. For example: *John has 5 apples. Ann has 2 apples. How many apples do John and Ann have altogether?*
Change events: A quantity changes from one value to another. For example: *John has 5 apples. He gets 2 from Ann. How many does John have now?*
Compare states: Two quantities are mentioned and compared in the text. For example: *John has 5 apples. Ann has 2 apples. How many apples does John have more than Ann?*

When a problem is read, a schema is retrieved on the basis of keywords, patterns in the problem text or the meaning of the problem text. A schema that would apply to the bottle of wine problem is the combine-schema. Note that this must be recognized from the problem text. This schema involves three elements, two quantities and the result of 'combining' these. Filling this schema gives:

Role in schema:	Name:	Value:
Result of combining	bottle of wine	5
Quantity 1	bottle	ASKED
Quantity 2	wine	?
Difference	wine − bottle	4.50

Note that the elements of this schema are essentially the same as those in the approximation method. The difference is that the schema is associated with procedures that compute the ASKED from the rest of the schema. For example, the combine-schema has the following procedure:

IF Part 1 is asked THEN the answer is: Difference − Quantity 2
IF Part 2 is asked THEN the answer is: Difference − Quantity 1
IF Difference is asked THEN
   IF Quantity 1 > Quantity 2 THEN the answer is: Quantity 1 − Quantity 2
   IF Quantity 1 < Quantity 2 THEN the answer is: Quantity 2 − Quantity 1

The procedure that corresponds to the schema application method is:

Procedure Schema application(in: text; out: answer):
1. Recognize schema (text; schema)
2. Fill in schema (text; schema; filled-in schema)
3. Find computational procedure (filled-in schema; procedure)
4. Apply computation (procedure; filled-in schema; answer)

The direct recognition method
Finally, it is possible, especially in a restricted sub-task defined by a particular class of arithmetic word problems, to follow a direct matching approach, the *direct recognition* method. Consider the sub-task of solving arithmetic word problems involving only problems with two numbers in the text that must either be added or of which the difference must be taken. This effectively means that problems must be classified as *sum problems* or *difference problems*. This can in principle be done from patterns occurring in the problem text. For example, if the final sentence is of the form *'How many ... do ... and ... have together?'* then the numbers in the problem must be added to find the result. If the form of the sentences is simple and standard then this pattern recognition approach is quite feasible although the rules associating patterns and solutions will be more complex than the example above.

In addition to these four methods there are general weak methods that guide problem-solving. Novice problem solvers, who do not know methods or strategies for solving such problems, or who do not have the knowledge that is needed to apply the method to a problem will use more general but weaker methods or they will mix parts from the methods that they know. For example, people who do not know appropriate schemata and who cannot in general solve algebraic equations will solve arithmetic word problems either by the approximation method perhaps combined with parts of the schema or algebraic method that they do know. Analysing this further requires more psychological knowledge about which knowledge people will have and takes us to construction of a psychological model.

The result of this exercise in task analysis is that we have identified four types of procedures for solving arithmetic word problems:

1. The algebraic method.
2. The approximation method.
3. The schema application method.
4. The direct recognition method.

Note that these analyses are still very far from completely specifying a model of the solution process. Some of the steps in the procedural models can be elaborated easily (for example 'solving a set of algebraic equations' or 'retrieving a schema') but other steps are likely to be very complicated. For example 'transforming the sentences of the problem text into algebraic equations' may be rather hard to elaborate. It may also be hard to specify the problem schemata that people retrieve.

We could elaborate these methods in more detail. We could even build initial computer models for them. However, it is a good idea to stop here and first present a different example of task analysis.

5.6.3 Example: task analysis of architectural design

The example is again taken from the study by Hamel (1990). He made a task analysis of architectural design by studying relevant literature and by interviewing 15 architects about their activities. He asked them for a description of their activities from the moment the assignment was given till the actual realization of the building. The main tasks of designing could be characterized as follows: gathering information, decomposition of design problems, solving the sub-problems, synthesis of the sub-problems and styling. For each of these categories he made a decomposition into sub-activities, distinguishing between the psychological aspects on the one hand and the involved knowledge and actions on the other hand. For example one of the main categories 'gathering information' consists of these activities:

1. The architect forms an idea of the kind of assignment he has been presented with.
2. The architect analyses the assignment by specification of the attributes.
3. The architect fills in missing information.
4. The architect checks the presented information.

To perform this task an architect needs to know:
(a) Which information is indispensable for making a design.
(b) The underlying wishes and goals from the respective clients for a great number of designs.
(c) Sources of information and the methods to gather more information.

This is a more abstract type of task analysis than the one we gave for arithmetic word problems.

5.6.4 The role of task analysis

Task analysis gives a first approximation of a procedural model. In particular it gives a first conceptualization of the range of behaviours that can appear in the protocols. Suppose that it has been possible to describe the knowledge and a procedure for applying it that can actually be used to solve problems. Perhaps it has even been possible to write a computer program that can solve the problems we are interested in. Psychological knowledge may now be applied to point out that certain knowledge is unlikely to be available to certain people, that they may apply other knowledge (that is not actually relevant or useful) or that the mechanism applying the knowledge differs from what we know about how the human mind works. From this psychological knowledge the task analysis can be modified to obtain a better approximation of the actual problem-solving behaviour. We call this second approximation the *psychological model*. Applying psychological knowledge will be described in Section 5.7 and constructing a psychological model in Section 5.8. This two-step method for model construction (task analysis followed by application of psychological knowledge) is the best method we know of in that it reduces the complexity of the modelling task. However, the model constructed in this manner is far from complete. Nevertheless, without an initial task analysis exploiting accessible sources about the task, constructing a model is much more difficult and one ends up mixing task analysis with 'data driven' modelling from the protocols.

The distinction between task analysis and psychological model and the two-step approximation of the psychological model is useful for both knowledge engineering and psychological research. In knowledge engineering the psychological factors may not be useful as part of the final model, in particular if they result in less competent behaviour. Think aloud protocols are then used to complete the task analysis with information about specific skills and tricks of the trade that cannot be found in textbooks and other sources. However, also in this case it is useful to take the psychological factors into account when analysing the protocols, even if they are not included in the final model. Consider, for example, the effect of practice. An experienced expert may not show the problem-solving behaviour that one might expect on the basis of a textbook or a training manual. From experience with the task she may have acquired special methods or shortcuts. This can sometimes be explained from psychological factors such as: experience with the task, capacity limits in the human cognitive system, 'slips' in performance caused by small errors in perception or memory, strong effect of recent events, etc. Another example is the actual context in which the task is performed. The architects in Hamel's study had access to their problem description, notes and sketches. The way in which these are used affects their behaviour. In this respect the conditions in which a computer system operates may be different. The architect may forget part of his original problem or he may incidentally note a useful idea in an old sketch. Both of these events cannot easily be accounted for by a task analysis as such.

5.7 Theories of problem-solving

5.7.1 The role of psychological theories

Thus far we discussed the first step towards a complete model: task analysis. The sources used for task analysis are accessible and rational. They supply the generally available knowledge about how a task should be performed. Nearly all sets of protocols are full of surprises if we compare them to the rational, well-informed way of performing the task. People behave in ways that are sometimes less rational and based on false and unexpected assumptions. However, they may also have discovered knowledge that has not been generally accessible but that allows them to perform better than the 'rational' task analysis can explain.

Psychology can supply additional knowledge on 'limitations of rationality' that make people behave in ways that are not optimal from a rational viewpoint. Unfortunately, most psychological research and the corresponding theory does not focus on cognitive *processes* but on properties of the result of performing the task, properties of the task and differences between individuals. This work can be used only indirectly to explain cognitive processes. For example, it is hard to say what properties like 'verbal intelligence' imply for solving arithmetic word problems or what differences in solution times between problems tell us about why one problem is more difficult than another.

Psychological theory contributes knowledge about the cognitive machinery and knowledge about what people generally know and can do (for example 'Dutch children over 6 years old can count and perform basic arithmetic operations'). In the task analysis, these kinds of knowledge are not taken into account. For example, the fact that people can only hold a small number of items in working memory may influence their problem-solving process in ways not represented in the task analysis. Human problem-solving behaviour is determined both by characteristics of the human mind, the knowledge that the person uses and by the task itself. In many cases there are limitations on the ways in which a task can be performed.

There are many theories of problem-solving. One example of a general theory postulates three types of process (Newell & Simon, 1972):

- Orientate
- Solve
- Evaluate

The orientation phase consists of activities that clarify the problem statement. It is characterized by asking oneself questions like: what do I know now, what is given, what is the problem, have I seen such a problem before, etc? All these questions are meant to derive extra information pertaining to the problem and its possible solution. The solving phase is characterized by the application of solving procedures (however incorrect these might be). The evaluation phase relates the solution to the original problem statement and is meant to check the solution for correctness or plausibility. Although these phases are very general indeed, they are specific enough to differentiate different behaviour. Beginners, people who are not familiar with the problem, often do not perform many orientation activities, and do not evaluate their solutions. Experts solve problems in the order denoted by the three phases. They often spend much time on orientation activities and they nearly always check their solutions.

Note that this theory on problem-solving abstracts from the task. It is applicable to a very wide range of tasks, from mathematical problem-solving to architectural design. The theory makes a prediction about differences between novices and experts at these tasks and these predictions concern the *process* rather than the result. In fact the theory does not even predict that experts will find better solutions: it *only* concerns the process.

Another example of a general theory is based on the notion of means-ends analysis (Newell & Simon, 1972). Consider the difference between the current knowledge and the goal and select a method or reasoning step that will reduce the difference as much as possible. This general idea has considerable explanatory power, especially if it is combined with a theory of memory capacity. This theory too abstracts from the content and structure of the task.

In our experience the most important elements in the psychological part of a model are capacity limits (in particular the capacity of working memory and of perception) and previously acquired knowledge. In most cases it is possible to obtain an initial model of the knowledge that people will use for a task by looking at relevant instruction and experience. This acts as a constraint on the result of task analysis, which is usually broader.

It is not possible to completely separate the psychological part from the task analysis. For example, the distinction between orientation, solving and evaluation has both a psychological and a rational background. The result of orientation is often necessary for actually solving the problem. This means that task analysis will tell us that orientation is necessary to solve the task. However, task analysis involves mainly the rational version: correct orientation behaviour that takes place at the best possible moment.

5.7.2 Example: psychological theories on solving arithmetic word problems

In Section 5.6.2 we gave a task analysis that consisted of several different strategies for solving a class of arithmetic word problems. We also sketched the knowledge that is needed to actually perform the task. Psychological theories that are relevant are:

(a) Special theories about arithmetic word problems which try to explain differences in difficulty between types of problems and differences between children's ability to solve them. However, there are few theories about the cognitive *processes* involved in solving arithmetic word problems.
(b) General theories about the structure ('architecture') of the human mind.

For example, one theory explains differences in difficulty between problems by the order in which schemata are acquired. This theory assumes a version of the 'schema application method'. Some problems are more difficult because they involve a schema for situations or events that children acquire at a later developmental stage. For example, according to this theory the compare-schema is acquired later than the combine-schema, which explains the difference in difficulty. Another theory focuses on the role of language understanding. Certain expressions may be misunderstood by children, which causes errors. For example, the problem text: *Mary has 5 marbles. She gives 3 marbles to Jim. How many marbles does Mary have?* may be misunderstood as meaning that Mary *now* has five marbles (even though she gave three marbles to Jim), which would give the answer 'five'. Also more general notions like 'orientation' can be applied here. This theory implies that children do not structure and integrate the information in the problem text but immediately look for a quick way to solve the problem. These theories can be integrated with the task analysis and will result in fairly detailed predictions about differences in behaviour between problems and subjects.

5.7.3 Example: psychological theories on problem-solving in architectural design

There are of course many psychological theories that have implications for the way in which architects design buildings. Here we shall follow Hamel's work that focuses on general properties of the human cognitive architecture. An important psychological factor in architectural design is the limited capacity of working memory. Architectural design involves a large amount of information as follows from the task analysis. Because the capacity of human working memory is limited and information is necessary for further steps in the design process, architects need to take measures to overcome this problem. According to Hamel there are two methods architects use to solve this problem:

1. They organize the information into a structure of smaller 'packages' (the 'problem conception') in such a way that relevant information will be accessible at the right moment during problem-solving.
2. They make notes and sketches which give a quick overview of the current design without creating extra memory load. Notes and sketches act as an 'external memory' and are accessed by looking at them instead of retrieving them from memory.

This psychological knowledge can be used in combination with the task analysis to construct a *psychological model* of architectural design.

5.8 Psychological model

5.8.1 The construction of psychological models

After discussing task analysis and the role of psychological theories, we now turn to the question how psychological theory and task analysis are integrated into a *psychological model* of the cognitive process at hand. The psychological model will be the basis of predictions about the protocol data. It summarizes what we know about how people will behave when performing a task. This means that knowledge about the cognitive mechanisms and about the knowledge that people bring to bear on task are used to modify the result of task analysis. When comparing the resulting model with the protocol data, discrepancies point to errors in our knowledge and unpredicted behaviour.

The psychological model describes the cognitive process that will take place in the context of a particular task, as implied by a psychological theory. The psychological theory may constrain rational behaviour as described in the task analysis, but it may also introduce new possible processes that appear, for example, when a person does not have adequate knowledge for performing a task.

Ideally, you would have a model that predicts what will appear in a protocol. In that case, it would be possible to generate a verbal protocol on the basis of the model. This latter case is very rare. Normally, the models used are somewhere between very loose and very strict. What kind of model one needs is partly dependent on the research question. If you want to test a theory, your model needs to be a proper operationalization of this theory. If you want to demonstrate global differences between two groups of subjects solving a certain type of problem, your model needs only to specify these global differences and how they might be reflected in a protocol, without specifying all problem-solving steps in detail. In the next paragraphs we will come back to the use of models and how they are constructed.

5.8.2 Example: a psychological model of solving arithmetic word problems

In Section 5.6.2 we sketched a task analysis for arithmetic word problems and in Section 5.7.2 we summarized some psychological research that is relevant for this task. Let us now turn back to the task that we gave as an illustration in Chapter 1. The problem that we gave as an instance of this task is:

Irene has 6 sweets less than Suzanne. Diana has 5 more than Suzanne. How many sweets does Irene have less than Diana?

This task was taken from a class of arithmetic word problems that all have the general form:

A has N1 'things' less/more than B.
A/B/C has N2 less/more than A/B/C.
How many 'things' does A/B/C have less/more than A/B/C?

So far the task analysis has given us four methods:

1. The algebraic method.
2. The approximation method.
3. The schema application method.
4. The direct recognition method.

Young children have not been taught the knowledge required for the algebraic method and it is therefore extremely unlikely that they will use it. This is also true of the approximation method although this is similar to the reasoning involved in evaluating the answer. This is something that children may learn at school. Evaluation is the first step in the approximation method and it may therefore appear in some form. Schemata are likely to be known by children at this age but probably not for this particular type of problem. It is likely that schemata for similar types of arithmetic word problems interfere with their reasoning about these problems. The recognition method is typically a method for experts in a domain. Whether children will use this method will therefore depend on the amount of practice that they have with this task. The subject of the example protocol in Chapter 1 had very little experience.

This suggests that a form of schema application is the best candidate. A more detailed model requires knowledge about the schemata and how these are applied. This is a good point to change the direction of our search from top-down (from refining a general model of the task) to bottom-up, inspecting the protocols to identify typical reasoning steps from the schema application method: schema recognition, schema application, selection of an arithmetic operation and computing the answer. Here is a first attempt:

Phrase	Interpretation/comment
1: so Suzanne has 6 more than Irene	transforms sentence; fits it into a schema
2: and Diana has 5 more than Suzanne	
3: so Suzanne comes first	suggests transformation to a 'X more-than Y more-than Z' schema
4: because Suzanne has some 5, er, 6	
5: but Diana has 5 more, even more,	keyword 'more' suggests 'add'
6: so altogether 11	operation suggested by keyword
7: but less is asked here	conflict with keyword cue
8: how many does Irene have less than Suzanne	
9: then you subtract that	'less' suggests 'subtract'
10: Diana, Suzanne, Irene	returns to schema
Experimenter intervenes	
11: [reads the problem again]	
12: I don't understand it ...	
13: Irene has something of which Suzanne has 6 more	
14: Diana has 5 more than Suzanne	
15: so something must be added	
16: and then something must be subtracted	operation suggested by schema; requires value of Suzanne
17: if I knew how many Suzanne had	

18: Suzanne has 11, I think   operation from
                                     approximation method
19: Diana has 5 more than Suzanne   cannot be checked
20: [pause] 10, I think
21: how many does Irene have less
    than Diana
22: I think 10

Individual steps in the protocol can be interpreted as steps from the schema application method. For example, several fragments show that a version of the 'direct recognition method' is used: directly recognize the computation from a pattern in the problem (e.g. lines 7-9). Other fragments can be interpreted as attempts to fill in a schema (e.g. lines 3-5 and 14-15). However, the knowledge that is needed to correctly follow any method is not available. As a result the subject encounters impasses:

(a) The question of the problem is of the form 'how many does X have **less** than Y' where the schema is stated in terms of 'more'. This confuses her.
(b) Although she can fill the 'X more-than Y more-than Z' schema this does not suggest an arithmetic operation. This may be due to interference from application of this schema to other problems. Most arithmetic word problems give the value of variables. The problem presented here gives only relations between variables. If the value is given, a schema easily suggests an appropriate arithmetic operation (even if this is not associated directly with the schema).

There is no easy way to resolve these impasses. The attempts in lines 4 to 19 are based on operations that are useful for solving other arithmetic word problems. Lines 13-15 show an attempt to apply knowledge from a direct recognition method (keyword 'more' suggests 'add'; keyword 'less' suggests 'subtract') and lines 17-19 show an attempt to apply knowledge from the approximation method. The subject guesses the value of one variable and then tries to evaluate the result. However, both attempts are abandoned because she evaluates them as insufficient.

This bottom-up analysis gives us some building blocks for a model. It also suggests several new sub-processes that were not part of the model so far:

(a) It is useful to include methods for similar problems in the model because these are likely to play a role even if they are not adequate for the current task.

(b) This subject does not follow a single method but mixes methods or rather parts of methods. The models that we sketched so far did not include this possibility. This is more likely to occur in novice problem-solving because novices by definition do not know a single adequate method.

5.8.3 Example: a psychological model of architectural design

In the next example of a psychological model, a psychological theory on problem-solving is combined with specific information from the task analysis. In Figure 5.2 the psychological model of architectural design, as developed by Hamel, is given.

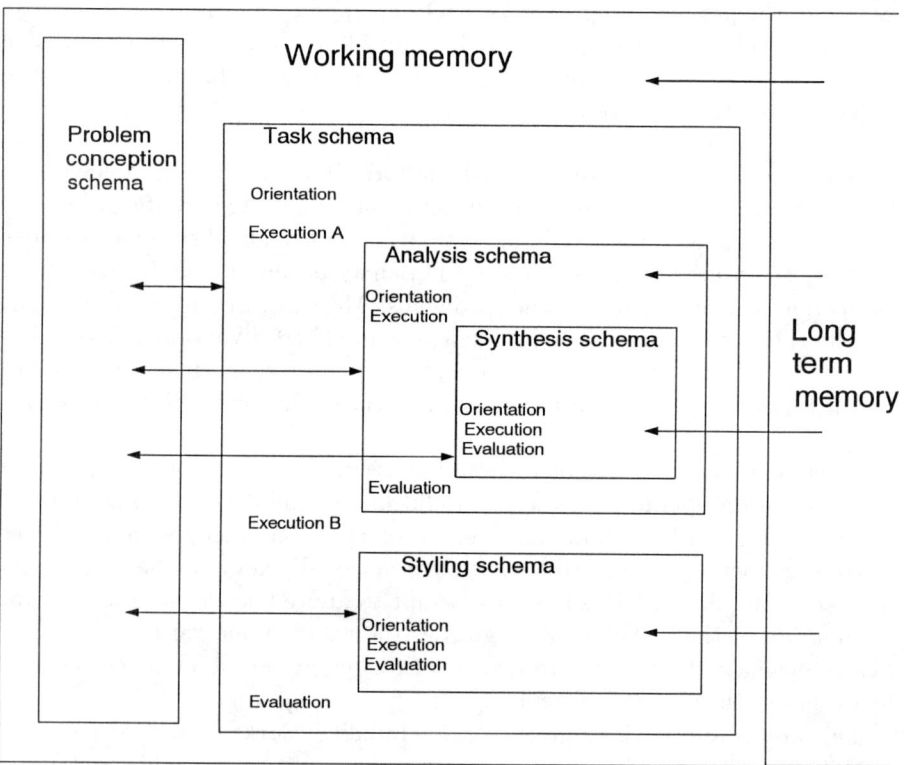

FIGURE 5.2: The psychological model of architectural design

The model is concerned with the design process, with what architects do and think while they design. Therefore the model is focused on what is called the task schema, which describes the procedures involved in design tasks. The problem conception schema contains all the information about the state of the design process. When the architect is given a design problem, the first thing to do is to orientate, which means to extract information from the text of the assignment. The actual work on the design problem is the execution phase. This phase consists of two sub-phases: the analysis of the problem and the styling of the solution to the problem into a design. The third activity in the task schema is the final evaluation. In the sub-schemata for the analysis and the styling phase the same divisions are found: orientation, execution and evaluation. In the analysis schema the orientation activities are: gathering information, decomposing the problem, and finding partial solutions. The execution phase of the analysis schema is further decomposed into the synthesis schema. This is an important phase because solutions to partial problems have to be combined to form one solution to the design as a whole. This sub-schema also is decomposed into orientation, execution and evaluation. The styling schema relates to the activities in the design phase where the solution found in the analysis phase is so styled that it meets architectural criteria. These criteria involve the aesthetic value of the design and the elegance of the solution: reaching maximal results with minimal means. So if the end product of the analysis activities is an intermediate design which meets the technical requirements of the client, the end product of the styling activities is a complete design which meets aesthetic and professional criteria.

For each of the general activities in the model, specific activities as found in the task analysis can be distinguished. For example on the synthesis schema level, orientation consists of re-reading the givens and making estimates on the combinations of design aspects. On the styling schema level, orientation consists of studying one's own sketches and making estimates on the outlook of the building.

The structure of the model as a whole is nested. The sequence of the activities during the design process follows from this structure. The model postulates the order of the four levels and within these the order of the three categories orientation, execution and evaluation. It does not postulate, however, the order of the activities within each of these categories. So one can predict that evaluation in a certain schema comes after the execution, but one cannot predict whether an architect first re-reads the givens and then makes an estimate or vice versa. It is possible to postulate the predicted order of categories of activities in terms of transitions between these categories. This leads to a matrix of admitted transitions.

For further details see Appendix E where all the specific activities belonging to the different main categories are listed.

5.9 Dimensions of models

Models may differ on a lot of dimensions:

Task-oriented models versus psychological models: The research question determines whether the model will be task oriented or psychologically oriented. If the question is the acquisition of knowledge about how a certain task can be performed then the model will focus on the problem-solving processes of experts, ignoring mistakes and inefficient methods. An example is a model of an expert performing a troubleshooting task. The goal is to acquire knowledge about how the troubleshooting can be done in order to build an expert system.

Task-specific versus task-independent: A model may be formulated in very specific terms which are only used in a particular task. An example is a model of solving a physics problem which uses terms like applying Newton's Second Law. A task-independent model will use only general terms, applicable to a wider class of tasks. An example of a task-independent model is a model using general terms like 'applying law', without specification of the exact nature of this law, so it can be used in several physics tasks, or still more general 'applying rule', so it can be used in all science tasks. Even a domain-independent model will have a limited range, over a number of domains. A model cannot cover all human problem-solving. 'Domain specificity' and 'fineness of grain' do not exactly map. Although very fine-grained models will often not cover many different domains, it is still possible to have a domain-independent model which is fine-grained, and to have coarse-grained models which are very domain-specific.

Process structure versus process properties: Although protocol analysis is always directed at cognitive processes, the main focus may either be *property* or *dimension* of a process (such as the proportion orientation activities) or the process structure: the sequence and conditions under which cognitive actions take place.

Scope: Some models cover, for example, the entire problem-solving process, where others only concern certain aspects or sub-processes. For example, a study may focus on how children transform sentences to equations in arithmetic word problems. Although complete protocols are taken, only a sub-process is relevant. This may not appear in certain protocols at all!

Individual differences versus general human behaviour: Models may deal with individual differences. An example is a model of how different types of individuals react to the same treatment. Models may also deal with how people behave in general. An example is a model of how people retrieve information when under strain, when they have to perform for instance several tasks at one and the same time. In the latter case the researcher is not interested in individual differences but in general possibilities and limitations of human behaviour.

Deterministic versus non-deterministic models: Task analysis and psychological model together may not specify a single possible cognitive process but a (possibly very large) set of possible processes. This means that it will not give a single prediction about what we can expect in a think aloud protocol of a person performing the task. Note that this is different from a model that predicts different behaviour depending on the problem data (or on the results of later reasoning). Such a model also covers a wide range of processes but it may still give a single unique prediction about each problem (or intermediate situation). Non-deterministic models specify a set of possibilities. This simply shows our ignorance. In psychological research this means that our current theory about the process is weak. It will be tested by checking if the protocols match at least one possible process. In knowledge acquisition, the knowledge engineer will use the expert's behaviour and the correctness of the result as the main criteria to choose a particular model. For reasons of explanation it may even be useful to elaborate and implement all variants.

Granularity: A model may describe the problem-solving process in very detailed steps. For example, a model of doing subtractions in columns may include all the different steps needed to perform the operation: selecting a column, reading the first number, reading the second number, subtracting the lower number from the upper number, writing down the result etc. The granularity of a model must be at least as fine as the psychological theory involved (or the level of detail required in the task analysis, if that is constructed bottom-up) and it must also match the categories one distinguishes in the expected utterances reflected in the protocol. A model with reasonably fine granularity is needed when all separate utterances made in a think aloud protocol are to be represented in a model. A model may also deal with broader categories of descriptions. For example, a model of the process of writing an essay will not describe every step an author may take, but will have categories like searching for new information, making notes, formulating a question. All these steps may take a long time and involve many different sub-steps. Another example is the solving of complex physics problems, where doing subtraction is only a sub-step of the category 'calculating'. Another possibility is to define (dimensional or categorical) properties of reasoning steps that involve abstraction. However, if the theory or the task analysis requires a level of detail that does not appear in think aloud protocols, the method is simply inadequate.

Distance to verbal data: The model may use terms which are more or less close to the verbal data in the protocol. Steps in the model like reading the problem out loud are very close to the data to be found in the protocols. Steps like orientation on the problem are further away, it is not readily seen that reading out loud belongs to this step. We will discuss these issues in the section on making a coding scheme in Chapter 7.

As we indicated in the descriptions, the choice one makes with respect to these dimensions depends on the goal of the study, the level of detail found in the protocols and the need for a computational model.

5.10 On the boundaries of task analysis and model construction

Difficult decisions concern (a) the *scope and depth* of the task analysis and (b) the *degree of formalization*. The knowledge that is potentially relevant is usually enormous for real-life problem-solving tasks. Architectural design, for example, may at some point require theories of human perception, heat flow and even more remote knowledge. Where to stop depends on the purpose of the task analysis. In the case of top-down psychological research this means:

1. Interpreting the theory of problem-solving in terms of the problem-solving task.
2. Finding a psychological model that will allow defining a coding scheme that is adequate for the problem-solving task that will be used in the experiment.

To decide if the second goal has been achieved, it may be necessary to try to define a coding scheme and test it on pilot protocols. In the case of exploratory psychological research it is more difficult to determine the scope of the task analysis.

It may seem that in the context of building knowledge-based systems, task analysis is putting the cart before the horse. The possible solutions, givens, possible solution methods, etc. are just what we need to know. However, in this case too it is more effective to start by a task analysis from other sources than think aloud protocols, such as textbooks. In this case the scope of the task analysis will be determined by the requirements for the knowledge-based systems instead of the experimental tasks. It may happen that an expert has unique expertise.

The example of a psychological model of architectural design that we discussed was rather informal. In psychological research it often useful to use more formal languages to formulate a model. In some cases it may even be useful to use an executable computer language and build an executable model. In the next chapter we discuss possible languages with examples of models of solving arithmetic word problems.

Literature

Theories and models of the way in which children solve arithmetic word problems are given by Kintsch (1985), Riley et al. (1983) and Sandberg & de Ruiter (1985). There are many possible problem-solving methods that can be used as the basis for models. Some of these are described in the Artificial Intelligence and cognitive science literature. See Patil, 1988, for an overview of methods for medical diagnosis and for example Mitri, 1991, for a discussion of methods for 'candidate evaluation'. See Clancey, 1988; Kuipers & Kassire, 1984; Kuipers et al., 1988, for models of medical problem-solving based on think aloud protocols.

Chapter 6

Languages for task analysis and psychological modelling

6.1 Introduction

A task analysis and a psychological model must be represented in some form, in a language. In addition to normal human language more formal languages are used for this purpose. In knowledge acquisition a structured, more or less formal language is always necessary, even if it were only the language in which the resulting computer program is written. Even though knowledge-based systems usually address only a relatively small and specialized task, they may require many different types of knowledge such as concept definitions, scientific theories, experience and rules of thumb. To make all this work together, to document the knowledge for later modification or for collaboration between people working on the task of building the system, and to make it executable by a computer, requires that it is expressed in a structured form.

In psychological research it is sometimes possible, and even advantageous, to avoid complex models by using tasks that are basically simple and involve little knowledge. This makes it easier to understand what people do when solving a problem. However, even rather simple tasks, such as puzzles, often lead to complex problem-solving processes, in particular when the person solving the problem has no routine, clear-cut way of finding the solution. In this case too, a formal language will help to formulate the task analysis and the psychological model clearly.

There are many different languages that can be used for this purpose. The choice of a language is not of decisive importance when building a model but an appropriate language will make the task analysis or model more concise and easier to understand. In the previous chapter we used language based on procedures and sub-procedures to formulate models. For some models such language is less suitable, for example because it is not executable. To formulate such models different languages are more appropriate. The most important properties of a language are:

(a) It must contain constructs that allow compact and clear expression of the important elements in a task analysis or psychological model. For example, if the model focuses on problem-solving strategy then the language should contain constructs for representing strategies, such as 'IF X THEN DO Y ELSE DO Z' or 'REPEAT X UNTIL Y'. If, on the other hand, the model emphasizes the representation of the problem, it should have constructs to represent, for example, structured objects, possibly graphical objects. In well-formalized domains it is usually possible to borrow the language that is used in the domain. For example, if we model arithmetic problem-solving, we use a formal language that is used to describe arithmetic procedures.

(b) Depending on the way in which it will be used, the language may have to be executable by a computer. Some formal languages are executable on a computer, which means that if a complete model is specified in the language, it can in principle be applied to a problem and executed as a computer program. Then it will 'animate' the model and simulate the behaviour that it describes.

The format of the task analysis and the psychological model for solving arithmetic word problems and architectural design was rather informal. This is adequate if no computational model is needed and if we want to focus on differences in procedures. However, we may want a more formal description or even an implemented simulation program, for example to facilitate analysis of the implications and assumptions of a model. In that case we need a more formal representation language. What language shall we use? A language that is popular in psychology is (linear) *algebraic equations* or *functions*. Several studies of arithmetic word problems formulate their model as for example:

$$difficulty(Problem) = g \times schematype(Problem)$$

where g is a number representing the statistical association between schematype and difficulty and where *schematype(Problem)* is the type of the schema that applies to the problem (see Section 5.6.2). More complex models take student properties into account, which would give for example:

$$difficulty(Problem, Person) =$$
$$g1 \times schematype(Problem) + g2 \times intelligence(Person, Problem)$$

This type of model is also used in building knowledge-based systems. For example, in a knowledge-based system that finds a diagnosis from a set of data on a patient we could look for a function of the form:

$$WeightedSum = g1 \times symptom-1 + g2 \times symptom-2 + ... + g3 \times symptom-n$$

and decide on a threshold for $WeightedSum$ to make a final decision. However, it is usually rather difficult, if not impossible, to obtain such weights. They cannot be found in the protocols and they are hard to acquire otherwise. This would also not give us a model of the cognitive process but only of the input and output of the process. Algebraic equations about properties such as schematype, intelligence and symptom are clearly an inappropriate language to express procedural models. More appropriate are special procedural languages.

Frequently used languages are: conceptual modelling languages, production rules, problem behaviour graphs and pseudo programming languages. In this section we will only present a few, frequently used, formal modelling languages. These languages are presented in a simplified form, for more complex and detailed descriptions we refer to the literature. However, even with simple versions, it is possible to represent sophisticated models.

In the context of this book it is not possible to present formal modelling languages in full depth. The purpose of the remainder of this chapter is to illustrate several frequently used modelling languages and to explain them with examples to a level at which you can make models yourself.

6.2 A conceptual modelling language

6.2.1 CPML

We start our discussion with languages that are more formal than just verbal descriptions, but that involve fewer details than for example programming languages. The first language that we discuss here, CPML (Conceptual Protocol Modelling Language) is a simplified version of a language that was designed for *documenting* knowledge in the course of knowledge engineering. The knowledge that is acquired by interviewing experts, consulting textbooks and other sources, must be documented before it will be used as the basis of a computer system. The KADS methodology (Schreiber *et al.*, 1993) for developing knowledge-based systems assigns an important role to the analysis of think aloud protocols. To be able to better handle the complexity of human expertise, the KADS methodology employs not one but several modelling languages. This allows a stepwise transformation between verbal data on expertise to a computer system. Here we shall describe a version of the Conceptual Protocol Modelling Language, the first level of formalization. The second and third levels consist of a formal specification language based on predicate logic and on more technical characteristics of the computer system. We shall not discuss these here but in the literature references at the end of this chapter we point to sources for this. Although CPML was designed for building knowledge-based systems, it is well suited to model any kind of cognitive process.

CPML distinguishes different *types of knowledge*. In many problem-solving tasks there is a useful distinction between descriptive domain knowledge and methods for problem-solving. In architectural design one can distinguish between on the one hand, the overall design method and on the other hand, knowledge about requirements, regulations, possible materials and structures of buildings. These are clearly separated in CPML but not in certain other languages as we shall see below. CPML relies on concepts that have an intuitive interpretation. It involves a structure of three different layers of knowledge. The first layer, the *domain layer*, contains the descriptive knowledge that can be used to reason from givens to solution (including useless reasoning steps). The second layer, the *inference layer*, describes the types of reasoning steps and the third layer, the *task layer*, specifies the conditions under which such types of steps are taken.

6.2.2 Domain layer

At the domain layer the descriptive knowledge about the domain is represented. For example, the domain layer of the architectural design task would involve definitions of concepts that appear in the initial assignment as it is given to the architect, the concepts and language for the design that the architect produces and all concepts, facts, definitions, rules etc. that play a role in the task. Examples of concepts are roof, door, entrance and various materials, costs associated with parts of the design, functions of parts of the design, ways of using it, risks associated with them, and stylistic properties. In arithmetic word problems the domain layer would contain descriptions of possible 'problem texts' and 'equations' and of the knowledge involved in the solution process.

In CPML there is no fixed syntactic form for representing descriptive domain knowledge. Forms that are frequently used here are *lists* of concepts, concepts structured in hierarchies or *trees* or IF-THEN rules. Representation structures that can be used to represent domain knowledge are *frames*, *tables* or *networks*. These notions are taken from computer science and artificial intelligence. We shall not discuss these notions in detail and we use them in an intuitive way. At the end of this chapter we give pointers to the literature.

To illustrate this we give a sample of the domain of a model of solving arithmetic word problems such as:

John has 5 apples. Ann has 2 apples. How many apples do John and Ann have altogether?

In this case the domain layer is represented in the form of concept definitions. In the example below these are: problem text, sentence, person, object and equation.

```
Problem text:
     a series of sentences

Sentence:
     Object-1 Action-1 Object-2
         where: Object-1 is a person
                Object-2 is an object
                Action is an action (has, earns, holds)
     Object-1 has Number Object-2 more/less than Object-3
         where: Object-1 is a person
                Number is a number
                Object-2 is an object
                Object-3 is a person
     ...

Person:
     John
     Mary
     Ann
     ...

Object:
     marble
     apple
```

```
    balloon
    ...

Equation:
    Var = Nr
        where: Var is a variable
               Nr is a number
    Var1 + Var2 = Nr
        where: Var1 is a variable
               Var2 is a variable
               Nr is a number
    Var1 - Var2 = Nr
    ...
```

The problem text can be defined further in terms of expressions that may occur in it. The definition of equation could be extended by other types of equations and of variables.

When formulating the domain layer one must keep in mind that knowledge at the domain layer must be associated with a knowledge source at the next layer, the inference layer. This means that structures at the domain layer must correspond to structures in the use of knowledge. For example, a model may say that there is a process TRANSLATE that infers an equation from a problem text. Here the TRANSLATE reasoning step uses problem text and equation. It must therefore be possible to define these concepts in terms of the domain knowledge. In addition to these concept definitions, the domain layer will contain rules that relate problem text to equations. These rules can be formulated analogous to those that we shall give in Section 6.4.3.

6.2.3 Inference layer

At this layer procedural knowledge is represented that is used to make inferences based on the problem data and the knowledge at the domain layer. For example, in the analysis of the architectural design task at this layer we will find knowledge for evaluating a partial design with respect to requirements, for proposing extensions or revisions, etc. The inference layer is represented as *knowledge sources* and *metaclasses*. Knowledge sources are procedures and metaclasses are the input and output of procedures. The inference layer describes procedures and their relations but it does not specify the order in which processes take place or the conditions under which they take place. The domain layer is connected to the inference layer in two ways:

1. *Metaclasses* are associated with elements in the domain layer. For example, the metaclass *equation* can be used in the inference layer and this means that an equation will appear at that point in the reasoning process. The connection is made by naming the metaclasses after concepts in the domain layer. Everything that belongs to this concept belongs to the metaclass and can therefore play the role in the reasoning process that is specified by the metaclass.
2. *Knowledge sources* are also associated with domain knowledge. The domain knowledge associated with a knowledge source is called the *theory* of that knowledge source. The knowledge in this theory is used to find elements of the output metaclass(es) from elements of the input metaclass(es). In our discussion we shall not distinguish between the knowledge source and its associated theory.

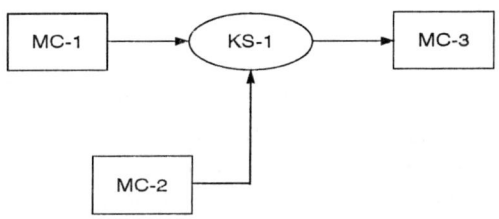

FIGURE 6.1: Knowledge source with metaclasses

For the inference layer a standard diagram format is used. Knowledge sources are represented as ellipses with the name of the knowledge source inside and metaclasses are represented as rectangles with the name inside, see Figure 6.1. This figure represents a procedure that uses input data from two sources, expressed by the arrows pointing into the ellipse and that produces one output expressed by the outgoing arrow. Each input arrow must either come from another knowledge source or it must be explicitly labelled as input to the whole process. Similarly, each output arrow must point to another knowledge source or be declared as output of the whole process. It is not allowed to connect two knowledge sources (i.e. without intermediate metaclass(es)) or to connect two metaclasses (without intermediate knowledge source(s)). This forces one to be explicit about the role of the domain knowledge.

An important property of a language is the ability to create abstractions, where details of a model can be hidden. In CPML language this is done by allowing a knowledge source to be elaborated in a *sub-inference model*. To keep the model coherent, the connections between a box at the higher level and its neighbours must appear in the inference model. Consider the example

Figure 6.2. Model-2 elaborates the *knowledge source* KS-1 in Model-1. Note that the metaclass MC-1 in Model-1 corresponds directly to MC-1.1 in Model-2. MC-2 in Model-1 is split into MC-2.1 and MC-2.2 in Model-2.

Model-1:

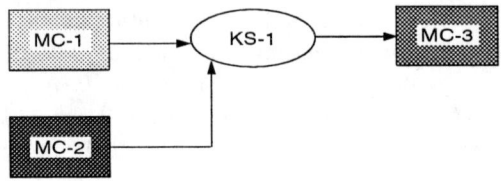

Model-2:

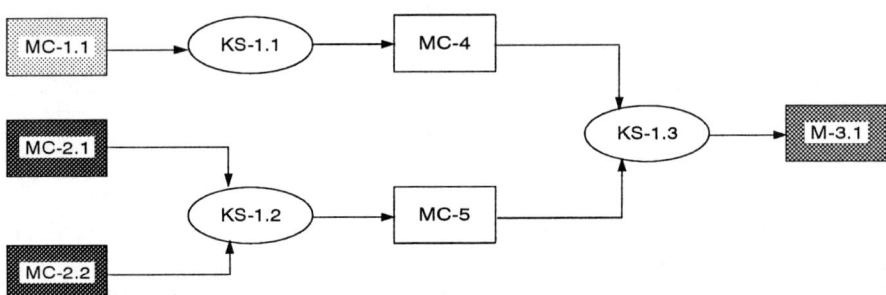

FIGURE 6.2: Layered inference model

To illustrate inference layers we give in Figures 6.3 to 6.5 three inference models for solving arithmetic word problems described in Sections 5.6.2 and 5.8.2.
Note that all metaclasses must correspond to terms that are defined on the domain layer and all terms on the domain layer must belong to at least one metaclass. If a metaclass does not correspond to domain concepts it is not clear which domain knowledge is to be applied at the reasoning steps described by the knowledge source. If domain knowledge is not associated with either metaclasses or a knowledge source then it is not clear for which type of reasoning steps it is used.

Also note that the inference layer does not fully specify under which conditions a knowledge source applies. For example, in the model of the schema

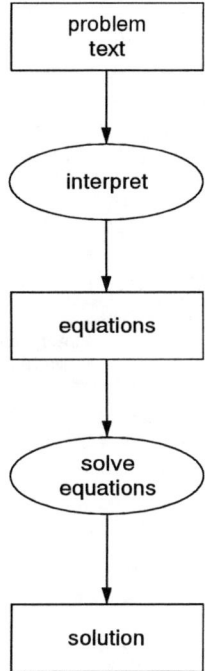

FIGURE 6.3: The algebraic method

application method (Figure 6.5) the *features* are used as input to both *recognize schema* and *fill in schema*. The diagram does not indicate which of these must be done first. This is specified at the next layer up, the task layer.

6.2.4 Task layer

The inference layer only models which processes need input from which other processes but it does not show in which order, how often or under which conditions (in terms of the data) a process takes place. This is done at the task layer.

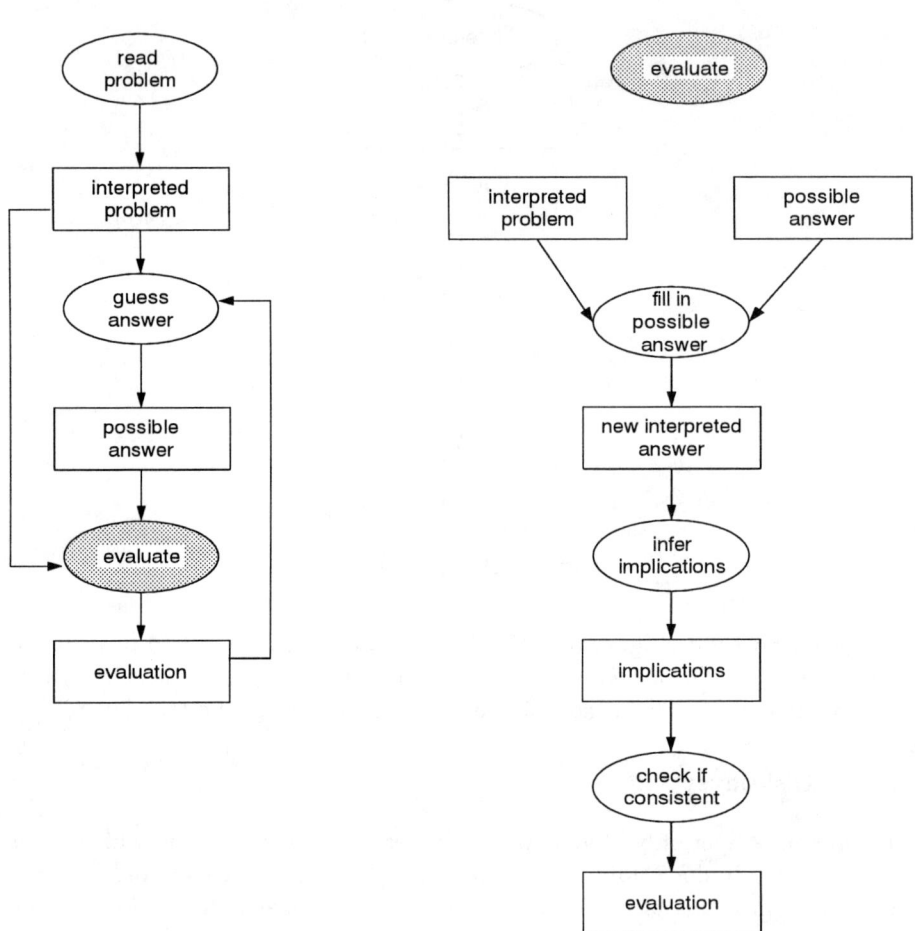

FIGURE 6.4: The approximation method

Languages for task analysis and psychological modelling 89

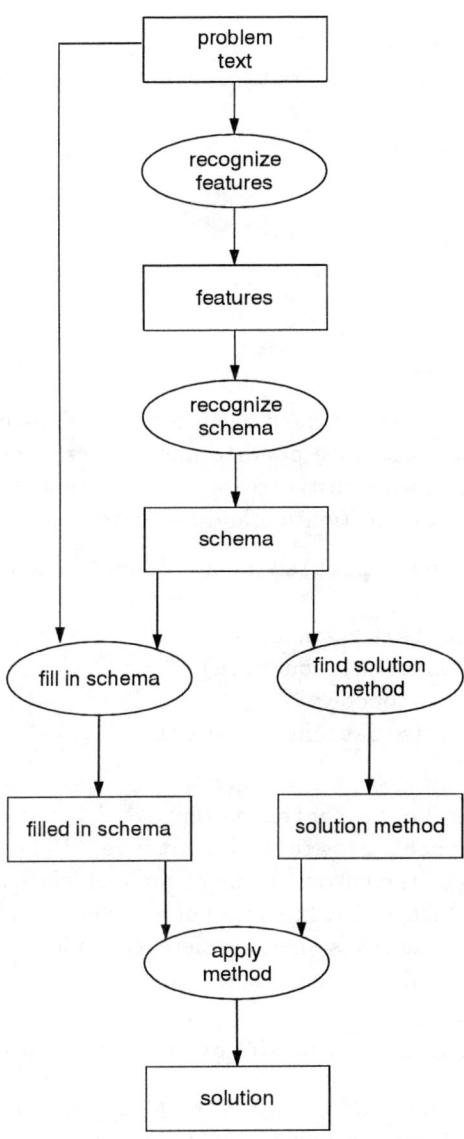

FIGURE 6.5: The schema application method

The task layer is expressed in a procedural language, using the following constructs:

```
Elementary procedures:
   knowledge-source(input: metaclasses; output: metaclasses)
```

```
Conditional procedures:
   IF     condition
   THEN   procedure-1
   ELSE   procedure-2
```

```
Iterative procedures:
   REPEAT procedure
   UNTIL  condition
```

In the task layer *procedure names* must correspond to names of knowledge sources, *parameters* must correspond to metaclasses of domain concepts and *conditions* apply to possible instances of these concepts. For example, the task layer for the schema application method could be:

```
Solve problem (input: problem text; output: answer):
  REPEAT
    Read (problem text, sentence)
    Interpret (sentence, equation)
  UNTIL no more sentences
  Solve equations (equations, answer)
  Write (answer)
```

Here `Read(problem text, sentence)` represents the knowledge source `Read` with metaclasses `problem text` and `sentence`. The condition `no more sentences` applies to the current value of the metaclass `problem text`. The knowledge sources `Read` and `Write` need not be elaborated here. For the knowledge source `Solve equations` another inference model can be formulated that has the same input and output metaclasses.

6.2.5 Example: a CPML model of architectural design

In this example we illustrate the use of CPML with a model of architectural design. Figure 5.2 shows the structure of the reasoning process. Here we elaborate the sub-process that corresponds to the *analysis* schema in Figure 5.2. This process consists of three sub-processes: orientation, synthesis and evaluation. In Figure 5.2 the *synthesis* sub-process is elaborated separately in the *synthesis schema*. These processes use information from the *problem conception*, the information about the current problem that has been collected and derived at a particular moment during problem-solving and they also use knowledge from *long-term memory*.

In CPML the reasoning processes correspond to knowledge sources and the elements of the *problem conception* that are used by a knowledge source correspond to the metaclasses. The knowledge in long-term memory corresponds to the knowledge in the domain layer. The model in Figure 5.2 does not specify the knowledge at the CPML *task layer*. Below we translate parts of the model presented in Figure 5.2 into CPML, we will present part of the inference layer (Figure 6.6) and also we add a possible task layer and examples of domain knowledge.

Domain layer:

• Metaclass **requirements**: Input to the analysis process are the requirements on the design. The form of these can vary over tasks. Here we only give a few examples:

```
functional requirements
maps and drawings
    geographical requirements
photographs
    aesthetic requirements
budget requirements
```

• Metaclass **structured requirements**: The initial requirements are decomposed into requirements for components of the design and the 'sub-designs' are partially elaborated. The 'sub-designs' concern rooms and other parts of the building. Examples are:

```
room
    livingroom
    meetingroom
    playroom
    garage
    bathroom
    cloakroom
    corridor
outdoor spaces
    garden
```

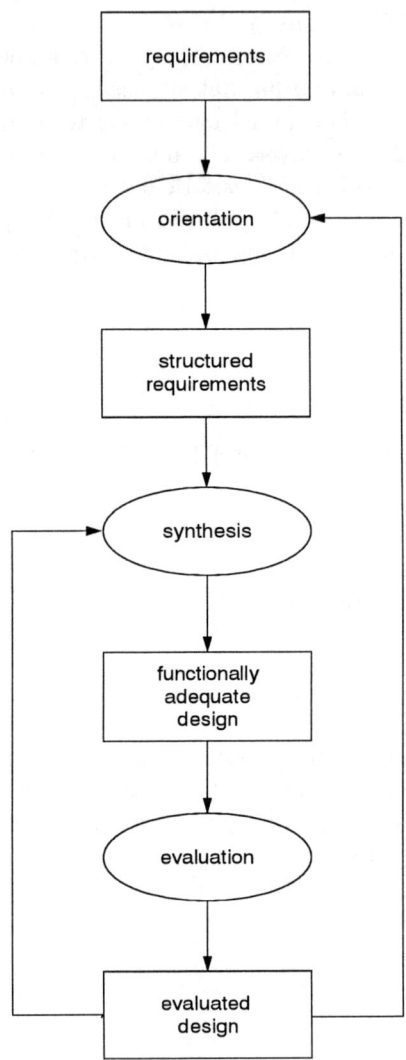

FIGURE 6.6: Part of an inference layer of architectural design

```
    playground
    access road
entrance
```

For each basic component design choices are made about properties of the component. Examples are:

```
Room:
    the approximate size
    the presence of windows
    requirements for pipes
    orientation with respect to sun
```

- Metaclass **functionally adequate design**: This refers to designs that are complete in the sense that they are composed from the partial designs generated above in such a way that requirements are not violated. The format of this consists of:

```
sketches and diagrams
    approximate measures
    sketches of floor plans
    sketches of cross-sections
    positioning in geographical layout
```

- Metaclass **evaluated design**: This is the result of evaluating the functionally adequate design in terms of the initial requirements to test if indeed no overall requirements have been violated. It consists of the design plus violated requirements (if any). This metaclass therefore refers to the same domain layer elements as **functionally adequate design** plus **requirements**.

- Knowledge source **orientation**: Below some examples of rules are given for **orientation**. The first rule represents that, if one of the requirements is a parking facility then one of the 'rooms' must be a 'parking space'. A parking space has several attributes (size, floor size, access, ventilation, fire escape) that will later on have to be established. The next rule states that if the 'floor size' of a parking space is unknown, the number of cars that are to fit into the parking space must be requested (from the client). The third rule represents knowledge for calculating the (approximate) floor size from the number of cars. The last rule shows a decomposition of a functional requirement into requirements for sub-functions (corresponding to required rooms).

```
orientation:

IF required: parking facility
   THEN ADD: parking space:
               floor size =
               access =
               ventilation =
               fire escape =

IF required: floor size of parking space
   AND number of cars = 'unknown'
   THEN REQUEST: number of cars

IF required: floor size of parking space
   AND number of cars = N
   THEN floor size = 2.5 * N

IF required: shop
   THEN ADD: required: shoproom
             required: storageroom
             required: coffee corner
             required: toilet
```

- Knowledge source **synthesis**: This contains knowledge for composing the building blocks into a complete design. In the model in Figure 5.2 this is elaborated in the sub-model *Synthesis schema*. To simplify the illustration we only give an example of synthesis domain knowledge.

```
synthesis:

IF required: parking space
   AND possible: basement
   THEN insert parking space in basement
```

- Knowledge source **evaluation**: Evaluate each requirement from the problem statement in terms of the functionally adequate design.

Task layer:

The task layer of this model concerns the choice to be made when an **evaluation** is reached. This is the only point where the model does not specify the course of the reasoning process and therefore the only point where a task layer makes sense. Depending on the content of the **evaluation**, the whole process stops or returns to **synthesis** or to **orientation**. Hamel's analysis does not specify how this is decided so we formulate a hypothesis:

```
IF there are no violated requirements
   THEN stop process
IF there is a violated requirement that involves only 1 component
   THEN return to synthesis
IF there is a violated requirement that involves more components
   THEN return to orientation
```

It will be clear that it will be very hard to elaborate this model in general to this level of detail. However, if the study is restricted to particular design tasks then it is possible to elaborate the domain layer for that special case. Of course this level of detail is not always necessary. The model can be kept more abstract and only refers to categories of processes rather than their detailed content.

6.2.6 Concluding remarks

The modelling language CPML is well suited for the analysis of protocols, because there is a natural correspondence between protocol elements and model elements as follows:

CPML	Protocol elements
domain layer	concepts/words
inference layer	types of transitions between concepts
task layer	conditions under which transitions occur

Conceptual models can be more or less detailed in their description of both processes and knowledge that plays a role in problem-solving. Less detailed models are expressed by giving only general domain knowledge and only partial domain layer theories. A knowledge source may correspond to a single protocol segment, a larger protocol fragment or part of a segment. In the latter case the analysis of the protocols is facilitated if sub-knowledge sources are defined that do correspond to a single protocol fragment.

Think aloud protocols normally consist of intermediate results of a cognitive process. They usually do not contain verbalizations of mechanisms that produce these results or of the (general) conditions under which transitions take place. That means that only the metaclasses (or rather their instances:

the actual domain concepts) of the most detailed knowledge sources appear in the protocols. The knowledge used for reasoning steps (the knowledge sources) must be able to reproduce the protocol data.

Conceptual modelling has proven very useful in practice. In some situations it is enough to construct only part of a full conceptual model. For example, if we are only concerned with the structure of the reasoning process and not with the domain knowledge, then it may be enough to only specify the inference model and the task model and not the domain model. This corresponds to the construction of pseudo programs. Alternatively, only the types of reasoning steps may be relevant and not the order or conditions under which they appear. In that case only the inference layer is relevant.

6.3 Pseudo programming language

The language that we used for the *task layer* of the models in the previous sections is a member of a family of languages that are referred to as *pseudo programming languages*. These languages are derived from programming languages like Basic, Fortran, Algol and Pascal. The difference with the actual programming languages is that pseudo programs cannot be executed. The syntax of the pseudo programming languages is usually less strict than the actual languages, constructs are used that do not exist in the programming language and datastructures are less well defined. Constructs, references to data and sub-procedures that have a clear intuitive meaning are not elaborated. The advantage over actual programming languages is that less care is required to formulate a model in a pseudo programming language than to construct a comparable running computer program in a programming language. That the model does not 'run' is sometimes not important.

Compared to CPML, pseudo programming languages do not have a standard representation that allows abstraction from the data and knowledge that are involved in reasoning processes. Examples of constructs in pseudo programming languages are:

```
IF Condition THEN Action ELSE
REPEAT Action UNTIL Condition
ASSIGN Value TO Variable
```

In an *ad hoc* defined pseudo programming language, the models of the cognitive processes in solving arithmetic word problems that we gave above can be formulated as variants of a general procedure. This highlights what the models have in common and where they differ:

```
Solve problem:
   REPEAT
      Read from problem text to: sentence;
      Translate (sentence, equation)
   UNTIL no more sentences
   Solve equations (equations, answer)
   Write (answer)
```

Variant 1: Algebraic model

```
Translate (sentence, equation):
   Parse sentence (sentence, parsetree)
   Translate to equation (parsetree, equation)
```

Here 'parsing' means finding the grammatical structure of the sentence. Elements such as the subject, the object and the action of a sentence are identified as a preparatory step toward translation.

Variant 2: Schema application model

```
Interpret (sentence, equation):
   Recognize keywords (problem text, keywords)
   Select schema (key words, schema)
   Fill slots of the schema (schema, filled-schema)
   Translate to equation (filled-schema, equation)
```

As the example shows, procedures in pseudo programming language can contain sub-procedures. It is possible that a model does not specify a single possible procedure but only several possible procedures. These alternative models can be represented by alternative sub-procedures.

Although this pseudo programming language resembles real programming languages more than CPML, there is still a significant difference between pseudo programming languages and real programming languages. Unfortunately, it is difficult for non-programmers to appreciate the difference between writing pseudo programs and writing real, running programs. We shall not try to convey this here but simply warn the unexperienced reader who believes that his or her paper and pencil model is almost a program that, in general, he or she is not even half way at this point.

The relation between pseudo programs and think aloud protocols is similar to that between CPML and protocols. Protocols show the intermediate results rather than the operations themselves. Variations in models appear as alternative programs. Here too, commonalities and differences can be highlighted by sharing sub-procedures and datastructures.

In general, we recommend using CPML unless the model remains very simple. The extra abstraction mechanisms in CPML are very useful for building more complex models.

6.4 Problem Behaviour Graph and production rule systems

6.4.1 Problem Behaviour Graph (PBG)

Newell and Simon (1972) formulated a psychological theory of problem-solving with an associated representation scheme. One of the key ideas of this theory is that problem-solving proceeds through a sequence of steps, each of which changes the knowledge that a person has about the problem at hand. When problem-solving starts only the problem givens are known. This is the initial *problem state*. Knowledge is applied that changes this initial state. In general, it adds something to the initial state. Problem-solving ends when the solution is known. The knowledge that is used to change one state to another is called *operator*. A solution process can then be viewed as a sequence of operator applications and states that starts with an initial state and that ends with a goal state.

The knowledge that people use to solve a problem is partially given in the instruction to a problem or to a general task and for the rest people use additional knowledge that they have acquired before. In most cases the knowledge that is provided in the instruction to a task can be translated into operators that can be applied to the problem givens, the initial state. However, in general more than one of these operators can be applied to the initial state. This means that the person solving the problem must decide which operator to apply to a particular problem.

In the framework of Newell and Simon this is modelled by making a distinction between the actual operators and 'control knowledge' for selecting an operator. The latter becomes the focus of interest, because the operators are derived directly from the instructions or from general knowledge. Newell and Simon introduced the concept *problem space* to describe properties of this control knowledge in relation to the operators. A problem space is characterized by:

1. States: States consist of the knowledge at a given time about the problem, such as the results of some part of the problem-solving process. There are two special kinds of states:
- **Initial state:** the state of knowledge in the beginning of the problem-solving process, such as the givens of a problem.
- **Goal state:** the state which has to be reached, such as the goal of the problem or the requested solution.

2. Operators: an operator is the connection between two states. When an operator is applied to a state, a new state is produced. For example, when an adding operator is applied to a state with two numbers, the new state consists of the previous state plus the sum of the two numbers.

Because usually more than one operator can be applied to a state, the initial states and the operators together define a graph. An actual solution path is a path through this graph.

6.4.2 Example: part of a PBG model of architectural design

To make this abstract notion more concrete, consider the following example of a partial PBG for architectural design. A problem state is represented as objects corresponding to the notions in Hamel's model (see Figure 5.2): problem conception, task schema, analysis schema, etc. There will be special operators that manipulate schemata (for example to create a new schema, to transfer results from one schema to another, to stop working on a schema and to start working on another) and operators that operate in the context of a single schema. The information that is used in architectural design is substantial and complex. This will result in very complex operators if an effort is made to express the full process in detail. An extra complication are sketches and diagrams that are quickly scanned by an architect. These processes are hard to model. In his study Hamel did not go into that level of detail. The following operators are therefore constructed to illustrate the use of PBGs.

Some example state descriptions:

```
problem conception:
   requirements:
      function 1:           price =              environment:
         name =             available space =       style =
         persons =          limit on height =       height =
         activities =       required materials =    colour =
         noise level =      ...                     ...
         floor scratching =
         ...

   current design:
      surface size =        playground:          building:
      expected price =         size =              size =
      style =                  surface size =      shape =
      drawing =                surface material =  material =
                               main colours =      colour =
                               ...                 map =
                                                   ...

         room 1:                  room 2:
            function =               function =
            floor size =             floor size =
            height =                 height =
            shape =                  shape =
            heated by =              heated by =
            windows:                 windows:
               size =                   size =
               shape =                  shape =
               colour =                 colour =
               material =               material =
            floor material =         floor material =
            colour =                 colour =
            number of levels =       number of levels =
            electricity connections =   electricity connections =
            gas connection =         gas connection =
            isolation walls =        isolation walls =
            isolation floor =        isolation floor =
            isolation top/roof =     isolation top/roof =
```

Languages for task analysis and psychological modelling

In the operators below objects such as `room 1` and `playground` appear as arguments. For example, the term `size(playground)` refers to the property `size` of the `playground` in the design. Some operators are defined in general, abstracting from the object involved. In that case the unspecified argument is represented as a capital letter.

Some examples of operators:

```
Op1: IF required function(X) = folk dancing
     THEN required floor size(X) = 80 sq. metres
Op2: IF floor size(X) = Y AND floor material(X) = wood AND
        Z = X * 120
     THEN price floor(X) = Z
Op3: IF required function(X) = folk dancing
     THEN design floor material = wood
Op4: IF required function(X) = folk dancing
     THEN design floor material = ceramic
Op5: IF floor size(X) = Y AND floor material(X) = ceramic AND
        Z = X * 200
     THEN price floor(X) = Z
Op6: IF persons = children
     THEN colours = {yellow, blue, red, white, green}
Op7: IF total-set(rooms) = RoomSet AND sum(prices(RoomSet)) = SUM
     THEN roomsPrice = SUM
```

Like Conceptual Modelling, this is a more abstract language than a programming language. It does not specify many details that would be required for a programming language. The PBG formalism has no fixed language for the states or for the operations that change the states. The language for this is to be defined. This can be a computer language but it can also be an informal, non-executable language. A knowledge state is intended to represent the knowledge that exists in the memory of a person who is solving a problem.

6.4.3 Production rules

Newell and Simon adopted an existing formal language that fits very well into this model as a more formal modelling language: *production rule systems*. Production rule systems are actually a family of formal and executable languages. These languages all share the following basic structure but they differ in a wide range of other properties. All production rule systems (PS) consist of production rules and a working memory (WM). The production rules have the form:

```
IF conditions THEN actions
```

The conditions test if elements are present in, or absent from, working memory. A positive condition is true if the element is in working memory and false if it is not. For a negative condition it is just the other way round. The actions are either ADD or DELETE actions, adding or deleting elements in working memory. Production rule models thus assume a mechanism that can perform matching, selection and 'adding' and 'deleting'. We illustrate this notion with a miniature example of a production rule system for solving arithmetic word problems by the schema application method. The model is designed for simple problems such as:

Mary has 5 apples more than John. John has 3 apples. How many apples does Mary have?

We need a few datastructures to represent sentences and schemata. We assume here that the sentences are represented as follows:

```
[<sentence number> <word number> <word>]
```

For example, the problem above would appear as:

```
[1 1 Mary]
[1 2 has]
[1 3 5]
[1 4 apples]
[1 5 more]
[1 6 than]
[1 7 John]
[2 1 John]
etc.
```

Once the format for the elements in working memory is fixed, it is possible to define rules that can apply to the content of working memory. Here are a few examples of production rules. The format for the rules is:

```
<patterns in working memory> --> ADD(element) or DELETE(element)
```

PRODUCTION RULES:
```
[? ? before]                              --> [ADD(change)]
[? ? now]                                 --> [ADD(change)]
[? ? loses]                               --> [ADD(change)]
[? X1 more] [? X2 than] [one-more(X2, X1)]  --> [ADD(compare)]
```

These four rules look for keywords in the problem text. If they find a keyword then they add the name of the schema that corresponds to the keyword to the working memory. The fourth rule does not look for a single keyword but for a combination of two keywords *more* and *than* that occur together. This is necessary because, for example, *more* by itself is not enough to recognize a schema. Note that here we need an extension to the language: one-more. In a programming language each expression must either have a special meaning in the programming language or it must be defined by the programmer. If we write these rules informally then we can be a little less careful here.

If the text of the example were expressed in this notation scheme the first rule above would add **change** to working memory. This means that it is a problem that is to be solved by the change-schema. Other production rules will have the presence of **change** as a condition which will have the effect that only rules that are appropriate for this schema will be applied.

The rules below fill a schema. For example, the change-schema consists of an **amount-before**, an **amount-after** and an **amount-change**. These are represented as three separate elements in working memory. These represent the amounts before and after the change and the difference. Two of these are given in the problem text. Once the change-schema has been recognized the amounts that are given can be extracted from the text.

```
[? X1 lost] [? X2 N] [one-more(X2, X1)] [change] -->
   [ADD([change-difference N])]

[? X1 now] [? X2 has] [? X3 N] [one-more(X2, X1)]
[one-more(X3, X2)] [change] -->
   [ADD([change-after N])]
```

The other rules fill the change-schema from the problem text. The first looks for a pattern ... **lost N** ... in a sentence and assigns N to the **change-difference** in the change-schema and the second rule looks for a pattern ... **now has N** ... and assigns N to the **amount-after** the change in the change-schema. For example, these the first rule would apply to the following sentence:

Mary lost 5 marbles.

and add the fact `change-difference(5)` to working memory.

Finally we give a rule for computing the answer:

[change] [change-before(N1)] [change-after(N2)] [N1 > N2] -->
   [A = N1 - N2] [ADD(answer(A))]

This rule computes A by subtracting N2 from N1 and adds the result to working memory as `answer(A)`. Note that this rule assumes both a special condition N1 > N2 and a special action A = N1 - N2 for computing A.

If the model now receives the sentences from the problem above as elements in its working memory, the rules given here can be applied and they will add new information to working memory. In the example above, the rules would add the name of the schema, fill the parts of the schema and compute the answer. Note that in a given situation, more than one rule is applicable. In this example, all rules add information to working memory. This means that at least we should prevent that the same rule is applied over and over. This is a simple example of the control problem that we mentioned above.

Programming languages based on production rules have built-in mechanisms for finding applicable rules and selecting one. Such a mechanism could for example exclude rules that double information in working memory. Such languages also have predefined structures for expressing elements in working memory and they have predefined special procedures. The way in which such predefined elements are organized defines the different members of the family of production rule systems.

6.4.4 Extensions of production rules

The basic mechanism of production rules (ADD, DELETE and matching the conditions of rules with the contents of working memory) have been extended in many ways to make it easier to express various types of reasoning. Here we summarize some of these extensions to give the reader an impression of the problems with simple production rules and also of the possibilities of implemented production rule systems.

Structured objects and variables: The example above contained only unstructured objects in working memory. Many applications require structured objects with production rules that access parts of the objects. One very common example are goal structures. Problem-solving may be modelled as reducing the goal of problem-solving (*design a building that meets requirements R1 ... Rn*) to one or more sub-goals (*design a building that meets requirements R1.1 ... R1.n, R2.1 ...*). The relation between these goals must be kept in working memory. A common way to represent this is as a stack. Production rules can have actions that test the top of the goal stack, 'push' an element onto the goal stack or 'pop' an element from the goal stack. These become special conditions and actions for the mechanism applying the rules. This would make it easy to model a reasoning process like:

```
so I have to find how many Mary has
well to do that I need to collect what is given
let's see, John has 7
he has 4 more than Mary ...
OK, now how many does Mary have ...
3
```

This reasoning clearly involves the manipulation of a goal stack. We leave the construction of the model as an exercise to the reader.

Another example of a special structure is the structure of the answer. The architect's design must also be accessed in terms of its structure. For example, reasoning steps will need *the rooms adjacent to room X*, or *the doors giving access to room Y*. Special productions that access structured data in working memory can be written for these operations. This makes it much easier to construct the model. It is possible to consider a special language for architectural design that contains predefined structures and procedures which simplifies the construction of a model. Here we list some important extensions to the basic production system architecture:

Calculations: The formalism above does not include calculation or evaluation of arithmetical functions. This can be added to the language by allowing special conditions or rules that involve calculating the result. There are several ways to realize this. For example, we could allow conditions like:

```
[annual-salary = X] [annual-interest = Y] -->
   [Z = X * Y] [ADD(annual-income = Z)]
```

Certainty factors: In some models the contents of working memory are uncertain. This can be represented by associating numbers with elements in working memory that express the degree of certainty. Think aloud protocols do not make it possible to infer certainty factors for conclusions, although they will contain qualifications such as 'likely', 'possible', 'unlikely'.

External memory: During certain tasks people take notes and refer to these during problem-solving or they use other media that carry information about the current problem. This can be incorporated in a model as an 'external memory'. This is similar to the standard working memory except that it is accessed by special production rules that 'read' information from external memory into working memory or that 'note' information from working memory on the external medium.

Explicit control knowledge: Hamel's model of architectural design had a layered structure. One level describes the various sub-processes of design and nested within this structure we find the content of the knowledge. This structure is not easily reflected in production rules. One way to express this structure is to define a production system with a two-step cycle. First a sub-process is selected and then rules (representing domain knowledge) are selected *within* the knowledge associated with this sub-process. Special rules can stop the sub-process and start a different sub-process, using information brought into working memory by the sub-process and other processes.

Rule strength: Some production rule models associate numbers with production rules that represent the 'strength' of a rule. 'Stronger' rules are preferred when more than one rule is applicable. This is especially useful in systems that learn from experience. The strength numbers then reflect how often a rule has been applied successfully and these numbers are modified on the basis of experience.

Parallel execution: A more recent variation consists of production rules systems in which all rules fire in parallel and the effects of rules are combined.

6.4.5 Problem Behaviour Graphs, production rule systems and human memory

There is a subtle but important distinction between production rule systems and PBGs. In a PBG a solution path may involve 'backtracking' to earlier (knowledge) states. For example, consider the structure of the solution process that is given in Figure 6.7. The numbers indicate the sequence of states. Now consider what happens to the knowledge of a person during this process. What if after S4 a subject returned to S2 and from there to S5? This seems contradictory. If S1 to S6 are the knowledge states, then what does it mean to return to S2? Does he forget S3 and S4? How can he return to S2? If we want to model this in a production rule system, how do we model this backtracking? The answer is to hypothesize special knowledge structures that keep track of the sequence of reasoning steps. Two structures are frequently used for this

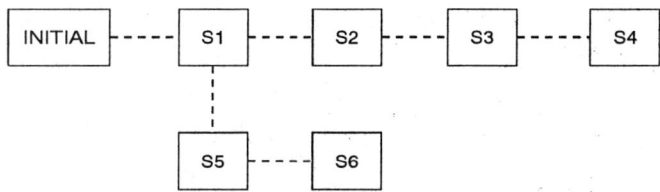

FIGURE 6.7: Example of a solution process represented in a PBG

purpose: 'stacks' and 'trees'. One possibility is to maintain a 'stack' of states that have been visited. If an operator is applied the new state is put on top of the stack. If no operator can be found to continue from a state, the process returns to an earlier state in the stack. An obvious possibility is the element on top of the stack, which was the element that was put there last: the previous state.

Note that it is also necessary to be able to prevent running in circles. If S6 has no possible continuations we may not want the model to consider returning to a previous state that would lead to S6 again (in the case we have reason to believe that people would not do so either). This means that the system has to keep track not only of its current path (with the stack) but also of the paths that it has explored before. This can be done by maintaining a *tree* instead of a stack. This tree represents the part of the problem space that has been explored so far. The stack or the tree is in working memory but is manipulated by standard procedures in the production rule machinery. Note that one need not identify the mechanism of the production rule language with the architecture of the human mind. What is 'knowledge' in the psychological model can be represented as part of the mechanism of the production rule language. For example, if one assumes that people have the knowledge needed to perform simple computations correctly, computations can be included in a production rule system as extensions to the basic architecture as we discussed above.

Another subtle point is the construction of new objects. Classic production rule systems did not allow the creation of new objects from old elements. They allowed only adding and deleting from working memory. A problem-solving operation usually cannot be modelled directly by simply retrieving and applying a production rule. For example, problem-solving often involves *constructing* a new element from existing elements. This construction requires a special mechanism for *matching* and *applying* a rule. A simple example are calculations. Constructing a sum and adding it to working memory cannot simply be done by retrieving the given numbers and the definition of sum.

To actually construct the answer, arithmetic operations are needed in addition to retrieval and matching. Another example, from architectural design, is extending a partial design with a component that is constructed from two parts, for example, combining a half-designed kitchen and a half-designed livingroom into a single half-designed livingroom with open kitchen. Both these issues may seem details but our experience has shown that they become real stumbling blocks when one wants to elaborate and implement a model.

We have discussed production rule systems in some detail, because they are very popular in both cognitive psychology and knowledge engineering. The examples also gave a small impression of the difficulties encountered in formalizing a model. Production rule models are quite comparable to PBG models. The correspondence is as follows:

PBG	Production systems
operator	production rule
knowledge state	content of working memory
initial state	initial content of working memory
goal state	content recognized as goal
reasoning step	application of production rule
control knowledge	knowledge for selecting production rule

There is of course a strong structural similarity between the architecture that underlies production systems and an approximate model of human memory. Newell and Simon elaborate the analogy along these lines:

Human memory	Production systems
working memory	working memory
long-term memory	production rule memory
memory element	production rule
problem-solving	selecting and applying a production rule
perception	take input from environment
action	change environment

This model is the same as the one we used in Chapter 2 to explain the verbalization process: thinking aloud means partial verbalization of (new) elements in working memory. It is a matter of debate how far this similarity goes. One advantage of this modelling language is that it is easy to include knowledge about the cognitive architecture in the model. For example, if we have psychological knowledge about the capacity of working memory or about the time needed to retrieve knowledge from long-term memory, then we can easily include these in the psychological model.

To see how architectural assumptions can be included, consider again the production rule model of solving arithmetic word problems. We can assume that the amount of information that can be attended to (that is, the capacity of working memory) is limited. When the limit is reached, elements will disappear. We need knowledge or assumptions about how this works. Suppose that we assume that information that has not been used recently disappears. To model this, we can assign a number to each element in working memory that indicates the time at which it was used. When the capacity limit is reached, the oldest element disappears and can therefore no longer be used. Candidates for this are sentences of the problem text that are not used for schema recognition and schema filling. It may be necessary to read such a sentence again to enter it into working memory at a later stage.

6.5 Programming languages

More and more researchers not only formulate a model on paper, but also implement the model in a computer program: a simulation program. All the distinguished steps in the model will be translated to steps or procedures in the computer program. Often the program is written in languages used in Artificial Intelligence such as Lisp and Prolog, but is also possible to use other languages or authoring systems. When the model is implemented, it can be run on a computer in order to see how it behaves. The behaviour of the program can be compared to the actual behaviour of the subjects. It is then possible to modify elements of the model to see if and how the behaviour changes.
The main disadvantage of building fully computational models is that this takes much more effort than non-computational models. Important advantages of building simulation programs are:

Clear interpretations: Constructing simulation programs forces the model builder to be precise. It is impossible to write a running program when the model is fuzzy and inconsistent. The simulation program provides a model which is defined in formal terms. This makes it clear what all the different elements in the model mean, how they influence the behaviour of the model.
Visibility of gaps and redundant branches: Building a simulation program makes it clear where there are gaps in the model. The program cannot run when there are situations which are not covered. It is also possible to detect, when running the program several times, which situations never appear or which actions are never taken.

Unexpected behaviour and experiments: Running a complex simulation program, using different conditions or problems, sometimes shows unexpected behaviour. This may be behaviour which is never to be found in subjects, showing the weakness of the model. However, it may give new insights in the problem-solving processes. It is easy to feed the program all kinds of variations of a class of problems, many more than would be possible to give to subjects. Maybe some problems will lead to other behaviour than predicted. This would be an interesting outcome asking for new experiments with subjects. Another possibility is to vary the conditions under which the model has to work. These may be extreme conditions, for example overloading the model with information or setting severe constraints, experiments which might be hard to do with real subjects. Doing experiments of all kinds with computer simulations is easy and cheap, while experiments with real subjects is hard, expensive and time consuming.

Often the main advantage in building simulation programs is not found in having a runnable program, but in the process of building it. Formalizing the model, debugging it, making extensions and so forth, often gives a lot of insight in the processes to be modelled. Sometimes, researchers will never finish the program, but the model they started with will be much improved during the process of designing the simulation program.

Of all the languages that we discussed there exist versions that are executable. For example, an executable production rule language means that the form of the information in working memory and the form of the rules is specified and a mechanism is implemented for matching and applying production rules. This makes it possible to write a program consisting of production rules, input data into working memory and start execution of the program.

The disadvantage of computational models is that they require very much detail. Usually a computational model requires more detail than psychology can offer. For example, in a production rule system, all production rules that match the content of working memory are retrieved. This is a simplification with respect to the architecture of human memory. Human memory may fail to retrieve knowledge that was retrieved correctly in a very similar situation. It is usually not possible to construct a computational architecture and model the knowledge such that all aspects of the human process are modelled in detail. The resulting unexplained effects will appear in the analysis (see the next chapter) and indicate the limits of our knowledge.

6.6 Using a language or adapting it

In the examples that we gave so far, formal languages were used directly to represent a model. Often it is necessary to extend the language or to define a new language usually based on an existing one. This happens when the chosen formal language lacks constructs that are needed for the model.

For example, consider the task of architectural design. This involves the manipulation of partial designs. Objects in the design are added, deleted, moved, made larger or smaller, made to fit other objects, etc. Suppose that we want to model this in a production rule language. A (partial) design will be a complex object, represented as a set of facts in working memory. Deleting an object from the design will correspond to the application of a set of productions.

A good way to construct such a model is by defining procedures for complex operations. For example, it would be convenient if we can define a complex production rule to DELETE an object from the design. This complex production rule would then contain knowledge about the details of the DELETE operation. This requires careful definition of this new DELETE production rule to make it work correctly on a variety of objects and (partial) designs. If it is possible to define this, then we have in a sense extended the representation language with a new construct. Defining a new complex procedure in terms of other procedures is called *procedural abstraction*.

Psychological models are usually defined in terms of complex constructs which makes this type of abstraction necessary. Note that this makes it possible to design a language to meet the requirements that were listed in the introduction of this chapter: it is possible to define appropriate language constructs that have a psychological interpretation. The resulting language is still executable because it is defined entirely in terms of the initial executable language.

Consider the following example. Architectural design can be viewed as goal directed problem-solving. A problem is defined as a set of requirements on the design. Problem-solving can now be viewed as constructing the design, where design choices are made on the basis of both the current partial design and the requirements. Now suppose that we want to use a kind of production rules to model the design process. In general the conditions of these rules will refer to the partial design and to the requirements. We can try to construct a model along this line. However, at some points architects do not simply add elements to the design but they revise previous choices because completing the design becomes difficult as a result of previous design choices. It is difficult to avoid violation of requirements that were satisfied by the current design.

Modelling this process can be done by adding special production rules that model each revision operation. However, a different possibility is to construct a general 'revise design' mechanism that finds previous requirements and checks if they are not violated by the modified design. This mechanism can be applied by invoking it and giving it the current design, the revision and the old requirements. This can be viewed (and realized) as an extension to the production rule language.

A more principled solution is to introduce explicit datastructures that represent requirements that have been validated by certain design choices and to create special procedures that operate on these requirement structures. These operations perform tasks, such as *selecting a requirement, finding a design choice that meets the requirement, evaluating a requirement on a partial design*. This results in the construction of a special problem-solving mechanism, a *requirement solver* that is constructed on top of production rules. The model can now be expressed in terms of requirements and the knowledge associated with the requirements, such as *select requirement*, etc. A new language has been defined in terms of production rules. Recent research in knowledge acquisition has resulted in a range of systems that are based on special problem-solving mechanisms and that are therefore applicable to specific reasoning processes. These systems are not only relevant for knowledge acquisition but also for psychology and education because they contain models of particular types of reasoning processes.

6.7 Differences between languages

The reader will have noticed that there are similarities between the languages that we discussed: the language for the *task layer* in the CPML is a pseudo programming language and the rules that can be used to represent the domain knowledge associated with a knowledge source can be production rules. For a particular model we therefore have at least the following three possibilities:

1. Use the CPML.
2. Use *only* production rules. This amounts to constructing only the domain layer of the CPML model.
3. Use *only* the pseudo programming language. Compared to the CPML model this amounts to expressing the domain knowledge in pseudo programming language. This model will consist of the task layer of the CPML model but the knowledge sources and their associated domain knowledge will now also be represented as code in a pseudo programming language.

Note that the last possibility makes it more difficult to use structures such as concept hierarchies and rules to represent knowledge involved in problem-solving. Using only production rules makes it more difficult to represent the structure in the knowledge because that will not be reflected directly in the model. We must add that these are not fundamental properties of the languages. It is possible, for example, to organize the rules in rulesets and to group these in the description of the model. However, the predefined structures in CPML support and enforce this which is helpful, especially in larger models. Important properties are:

Executable: Are there computer systems that can actually run models specified in this type of language?
Control structures: Another important aspect of cognitive processes is the order in which processes take place and the conditions under which one action takes place instead of another that was also possible. For example, in the architectural design task it was noted by Hamel that architects first construct a design that meets the functional requirements and then refine this to achieve a particular style or aesthetic accent. This could also have been done in an early stage or after finishing part of the design. This phenomenon is difficult to model by production rules, because it is not easy to specify the conditions under which *aesthetic rules* are to be applied.
Deterministic or not: Production rule models make it easy to specify models that are non-deterministic with respect to control knowledge. This can be an advantage if the conditions under which a sub-process takes place are only partially known. This partial knowledge can easily be reflected in an undeterministic production rule model.
Assumptions about the cognitive mechanism: Production rule systems have an underlying mechanism, the architecture, which resembles the human cognitive system. This makes it easier than with other languages to include assumptions about the architecture in the model.

The characterizations below apply only to the languages that we sketched here. There are many variations of for example production rules and conceptual modelling languages and these differ with respect to the properties in this comparison.

	CPML	Pseudo programming languages	PBG/ production rules
Executable	no	nearly	possible
Control structures	yes	yes	possible
Deterministic about control	optional	yes	optional
Including assumptions about mechanism	hard	very hard	easy

Literature

Our language CPML is based on the KADS modelling language (KCML). CPML is somewhat simplified (for more details, consult the references at the end of this section). The most important difference between KCML and CPML is that CPML has no restricted set of knowledge sources. The original KCML has a set of predefined knowledge sources that describe types of problem-solving steps. Research in the context of this modelling language has produced a library of models defined in terms of these knowledge sources that can be used as the basis for constructing new models. Another difference is that we have omitted a fourth layer of the KCML model, the *strategic layer*. The best references on the KADS methodology can be found in the book by Schreiber et al. (1993) and in several articles. More specifically Wielinga et al. (1992) give an overview of the KADS methodology, van Harmelen & Balder (1992) describe the logic-based formal specification language $(ML)^2$ and Breuker & Wielinga (1987) discuss the use of think aloud protocols in the KADS methodology. Several systems have been built by designing and implementing a new language. For example, the PDP system (Jansweijer *et al.*, 1987; Jansweijer, 1988) which combines concept hierarchies and goal oriented production rules and was written on top of Prolog. Brownstone et al. (1985) discuss production rule systems. Another implemented system based on production rules is SOAR (Laird et al. 1987). Newell & Simon (1972) provide an excellent and extensive discussion with examples of problem behaviour graphs and production rule models. Lucas & van der Gaag (1991) give a detailed technical discussion of production rule systems. Another psychologically motivated language based on production rules is the GRAPES system by Anderson and his colleagues (1989). A collection of special purpose problem-solving mechanisms developed for knowledge acquisition is Marcus (1988). Musen (1989a, 1989b) describes a more general method for designing special purpose problem solvers along with support tools.

Chapter 7

Analysing the protocols

7.1 Introduction

Thus far we have discussed how think aloud protocols are collected and how psychological models are constructed. We now turn our attention to the relation between the protocols and the psychological model. There are three issues that deserve attention in the analysis of think aloud protocols:

1. Constructing a mapping between protocols and model.
2. Avoiding bias and interpretation errors in comparing protocols and model.
3. Quantifying the correspondence between protocols and model.

This chapter will give standard procedures and techniques for the analysis process. Figure 7.1 lists the steps of this phase of protocol analysis. The goal is to construct a mapping between the psychological model and how the cognitive process will appear in the protocols. This mapping will take the form of a coding scheme that is based on the psychological model and a *verbalization theory*: a theory about the verbalization process. Using this, the protocol can be compared with the model. We shall describe how to construct a coding scheme and how to apply this in the context of psychological research. Finally we go into the comparison of the coded protocol with the constructed model. This chapter will be concluded by making suggestions on how to report the results of studies using protocol analysis.

In the context of knowledge acquisition objective measurement of the correspondence between protocol and model is less important than in empirical research. However, also the knowledge engineer has to specify the relation

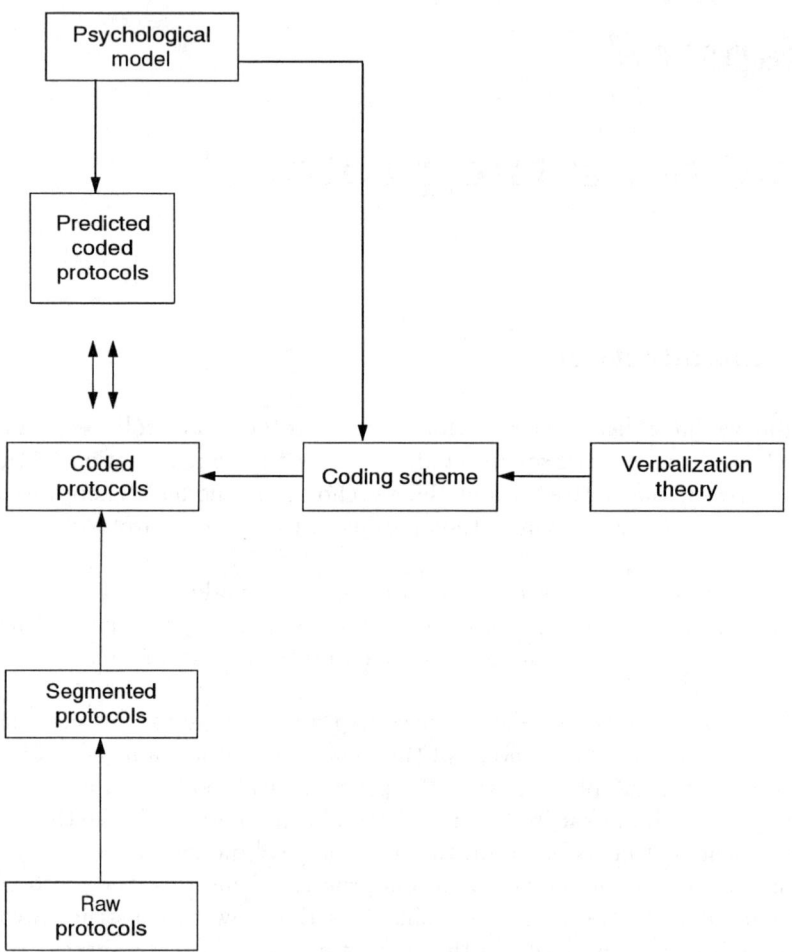

FIGURE 7.1: The analysis process

between protocols and model but it is not necessary to take measures to avoid bias in the interpretation or to quantify the correspondence between protocol and model. Therefore Sections 7.5 to 7.7 (Coding procedures, Intercoder reliability and Comparing the coded protocols with the models) and 7.9 (Reporting the results of protocol analysis) are less relevant for the reader who is only interested in knowledge acquisition. Both in knowledge acquisition and in scientific research a mapping between protocols and model is constructed. Therefore the rest of this chapter is relevant for both applications.

7.2 The role of protocols as data in research

In scientific research a distinction can be made between 'raw data', 'data' and 'theory'. Raw data are obtained by measuring procedures that are objective in the sense that they can be applied under any condition and will produce the same results. These results are generally considered as valid by the scientific community. Examples of such standard procedures are the use of certain thermometers to measure the temperature, the use of electronic clocks and hand-switches to measure reaction times and the use of certain intelligence tests and procedures for administering these. In some cases these objective data are interpreted, abstracted or aggregated in a way that is not as objective as the previous procedures. For example, the scores on an intelligence test may be combined to measure a new type of intelligence or time measurements are classified as indicators of a cognitive style by human judgment. In that case the result is less objective because it may depend on human judgment or because its validity is not generally accepted.

In the context of think aloud protocols we give standardized procedures for *segmenting* the written protocols and we argue that segmented protocols can be treated as *raw data*. The next step from raw data to the model is to *code* the segments in terms of the model. This usually requires a *coding scheme*, an extension to the model that describes how categories of the model will appear in the protocol. The *coded protocols* are *data* in the sense that coding involves procedures and coding schemes that are less objective than those for segmenting. The *coded protocol* that can be compared with the model which is directly derived from the theory.

7.3 Transcription and segmentation

It is very hard to analyse a think aloud protocol directly from audio recording. This is especially so in exploratory use of protocols. It is simply more difficult to get an overview over audio recordings and it is also more difficult to retrieve fragments from an audio recording. Protocols are generally transcribed into text. Although we may hope that in the future this process can be automated it is now simply much work. Transcribing is easier when using a special cassette player with a foot-switch and much depends on the quality of the recording. Notes and other observations are inserted in the transcription as much as possible.

Next the protocol is *segmented*, that is divided into *segments*. Research on language production and language understanding shows that in speech the boundaries of phrases are usually marked by pauses (Ericsson & Simon, 1993). The combination of these pauses and the linguistic structure provide a natural and general method to segment a think aloud protocol. Experience with segmentation has shown that there generally exists a high level of agreement between people asked to segment a written protocol while listening to it. Segmentation becomes more difficult and less reliable when it is done on the basis of the written text only. It is a good idea to design a form for the protocol segments and the analysis and to number the segments on this form. There are many computer systems that can be used to support storing and retrieving protocol fragments. Segments can for example become items in a database and be indexed by information about the protocol (subject, problem, date, etc.) and by model categories. In the analysis, segments are often combined into *episodes*, see Section 7.5.2. An episode is a sequence of segments that corresponds to a single element in the model.

7.4 Coding scheme and verbalization theory

7.4.1 Introduction

A procedural psychological model describes *which* cognitive processes will occur and also *in which order* they will occur. There is often still a substantial gap between the model and the protocol data. This makes it necessary to extend the model with an *operational definition* of categories in the model in the form of a coding scheme. The coding scheme specifies how elements of the model can be identified in the data. In the context of knowledge acquisition it is also relevant to consider this question because the verbalization theory will tell the knowledge engineer which information can be obtained directly from the protocols, which cannot be obtained at all and which can be obtained partially or indirectly. In the context of knowledge engineering a coding scheme is not necessary to achieve objective data analysis but is used for retrieval of relevant protocol fragments. In practice one usually associates protocol fragments with model components without a mediating coding scheme.

7.4.2 Constructing a coding scheme

Because it is difficult and therefore unreliable to compare the protocol and the psychological model directly, it is usually necessary to make a coding scheme to help in the analysis. A coding scheme is based on the psychological model and and on the verbalization theory. The step from psychological model to coding scheme is usually quite straightforward. Take every (sub-)process distinguished in the model and state how you expect these processes to appear in the protocols. Take for example the word problem solving processes. The model for using the approximation method has a sub-process called 'guessing'. One could assign the coding category 'guessing' to this sub-process, and one would expect to find statements in the protocol indicating a numerical solution with a certain uncertainty. The subject will for example say: 'Maybe it is X (X = number)', 'Could it be X?' or 'Let's try X'. This would appear in a coding scheme as:

Cognitive process	Description
Guessing	'Maybe it is X (where X is a number)', or 'Could it be X?' or 'Let's try X'.

For every process described in the model one defines the *type of statement* referring to that process. Categories in the coding scheme can be described in general terms but it is usually very helpful to give some examples of prototypical statements for each category. If two or more categories are similar it helps to emphasize the difference. It is of course possible that it appears to be unfeasible to define a reliable coding scheme. In that case one can has to drop the distinction, to revise the conditions under which the data were collected or even to find a different method for collecting data.

This type of analysis of verbal reports is similar to *content analysis*. Content analysis is usually applied to written documents that are stated in grammatically correct language, which simplifies the analysis. However, content analysis has also been applied to, for example, interview texts, which brings it quite close to the analysis of think aloud protocols. The main difference between content analysis in general and the analysis of think aloud protocols is that the latter usually involve problem-solving processes and therefore involve process models. Content analysis usually concerns static properties of texts.

7.4.3 Grain size and aggregation

If the task analysis and the psychological model are very detailed then elements of the psychological model may correspond directly to segments in the protocol. However, often the model is more coarse-grained and a single element (for example a single knowledge source or production rule) corresponds to a sequence of several segments. This has no consequences for the coding scheme, because one simply defines categories that cover more than one segment.

7.4.4 Special coding categories

There are some categories in the coding scheme which are not directly derived from the model. These are the verbalizations which are not covered by the model, but may still be anticipated in the protocols. For example:

(a) Talking about not-task related issues ('Oh, I must not forget to call my friend').
(b) Evaluation of the task or task-situation at a meta-level ('It is tiring to talk so much', 'I hate these kinds of problems').
(c) Comments on oneself ('I am thirsty', 'I am not comfortable').
(d) Silent periods. At times people will briefly stop verbalizing. After some time they may continue or they may be prompted to continue. It may be relevant to assign a code to relatively long pauses.
(e) Actions. The subject performs an action (for example, writes a note or manipulates a device). It is usually best to include this in the coding scheme.

In some cases one would ignore all these events as irrelevant - because they do not bear upon task performance - so putting them in one category: 'irrelevant comments'. At other times, however, these remarks might be an indication of the level of difficulty of a sub-task or of the cognitive load of the subject. For example, if a subject makes a lot of task-irrelevant remarks each time he must do a calculation, one might suspect calculating is difficult for this person. Sometimes the content of these interruptions in task performance is not relevant, but the moment at which they occur is. For example, it may indicate that the person who solves the problem does not make progress (reached an 'impasse'). In that case, special codes should be used for interruptions.

7.4.5 Coding form

To facilitate the coding process, design a coding form that consists of the segmented protocol (with numbers for the segments) and has space for marking the code assigned to each segment and for indicating discrepancies between model and coded protocol. If the protocols are stored in a computer database this information should be added for each segment or episode.

7.4.6 Example: a coding scheme for architectural design

Let us take a look at a part of the coding scheme for architectural design constructed by Hamel (1990). This coding scheme corresponds directly to the model in Figure 5.2. For every category in this model several processes are distinguished. Take, for instance, an architect whose cognitive process at a certain moment is hypothesized to be taking place on the 'the styling schema level, execution phase'. Hamel states that this process should be reflected in the protocol as comments on the strategy and the way of working during the synthesis of the design. Such comments are, for example, verbalized in the protocol as: 'Well, I am now going to look at the consequences of this location for the playing possibilities of the kids and their safety.' Below we give examples of a few coding categories. The complete coding scheme is reproduced in Appendix E.

Code	Description
SO2	Synthesis, orientation, estimation of combining aspects of the design
AO2-10	Analysis, orientation, using one's own knowledge with regard to functions of the assignment
SU9	Synthesis, execution, isometric perspective
SE1	Synthesis, evaluation, comparison with expectations, inspection, or checking of data or requirements

These coding categories clearly require knowledge about the task. Let us now take a look at a part of the protocol fragment given in Chapter 1 to see how this was coded.

Code	Line	Protocol text
SO2	12:	but maybe we can with er do something with that shack
AO2-10	13:	water I'll just put tap [notes 'tap']

AO2-10	14:	what children of course
AO2-10	15:	what what what is much handier
SU9	16:	[sketches water tub]
SU9	17:	maybe something er where water comes out of er
SU9	18:	and that you turn off in winter
SU9	19:	but then it does not trouble you
SU9	20:	and then it may run into here somewhere
SE1	21:	then they can still mess about ... with water
SE1	22:	then they can play with this
SE1	23:	that just comes it slowly drips out of it or so
SE1	24:	then they'll get dripping wet in summer
SE1	25:	and then they can get around this

Note that here each segment is coded. An alternative way to code this part of the protocol is to divide the protocol into episodes and assign a code to each episode. In that case, line 13-15 would be coded as `AO2-10`, line 16-20 would be coded as `SU9` and line 21-25 as `SE1`.

7.4.7 Verbalization theory

A coding scheme is based on the psychological model and on our knowledge of the way in which cognitive processes will be verbalized. In Chapter 2 we discussed the factors that influence verbalization. In particular, information that resides in working memory for a very short time, that is difficult to verbalize because of complexity or because of its non-verbal character, may not appear in a protocol. For example, a chess master analysing a chess position may well perceive a large part of the chess board as a whole. Verbalizing this requires her to construct a short linear representation that can be uttered as spoken language. This task is very hard and likely to give synchronization problems between the speed of the thought process and verbalization.

If verbalization is difficult, then verbalizations will be idiosyncratic: there will be individual differences in verbalization, even if the content of the cognitive process would be the same. Take for example tasting wine. Unexperienced wine-tasters when asked to compare different wines will talk of the flavour of the wines in their own terms, calling a taste sour or bitter. Expert wine tasters share a common vocabulary to express how wine tastes, calling the wine fruity. Idiosyncratic expressions cannot be covered by a *verbalization theory* and a coding scheme. In some cases it is possible to use part of the protocol to construct a 'personal coding scheme' for each subject. This is a good way to handle systematic differences in vocabulary between subjects. If a task involves information that is hard to verbalize then the analysis should allow incomplete verbalization and use a more abstract (or more branched) coding scheme.

7.4.8 Example of a verbalization theory

Consider the models of solving arithmetic word problems discussed in Chapter 5 and 6. Suppose that the persons solving these problems are reasonably experienced in this kind of task. What can we expect to find in the protocols? According to the model of Chapter 2, people verbalize the new contents of working memory or rather part of that. From the model we can find which information will appear in working memory. In the case of production rule models this is simply the information added by the rules and for the other languages the new information that is constructed during problem-solving is likely to appear there. For example, for the production rule model sketched in Section 6.4.3 we would find the following elements that can appear in working memory:

- The problem text (when it is read by the subject).
- Names of schemata (for example *change* and *compare*).
- Parts of schemata (for example in the *change-schema* we have: *amount-before*, *amount-after* and *amount-change*. These are either filled from the problem text or by computation).

For some expressions it is not clear if they will appear in the protocol. For example, according to the production rule model the name of a schema will be added to working memory. However, it is quite possible that schema recognition takes place implicitly and that the result does not appear in the protocols. This is plausible if there is no standard word for the *change-schema* and on the other hand this refers to the rather common concept of losing or obtaining something. This means that it is likely that people will not report this thought: it will pass very quickly and is relatively difficult to verbalize. From such considerations we can drop part of the list of possible verbalizations. This can be indicated in the coding scheme ('will/may not appear in protocol'). For the same reason the names of parts of schemata are unlikely to appear in a protocol. We will expect only the amounts.

Note that the production rules themselves do not appear in working memory. They are retrieved and applied by the cognitive machinery of the subject and do not appear as contents in working memory.

How sophisticated and elaborate should the verbalization theory be? In most cases there is simply not enough psychological knowledge and knowledge about the people involved in the task to predict what will appear in the protocol. This means that one has to resort to pilot protocols. These are used to perform the exercise described above.

7.4.9 Methodological requirements for the coding scheme

The main requirement for a coding scheme is that it allows objective coding of protocol fragments in terms of the psychological model. This breaks down into the following specific requirements:

Completeness (with respect to the model): The coding scheme must contain descriptions of all reasoning steps (or their results) that appear in the model and that can be expected to appear in the protocols on the basis of the verbalization theory. We should of course not require the coding scheme to cover all of the protocols. This coverage is the hypothesis that is to be validated. Segments (or episodes) that cannot be coded correspond to cognitive sub-processes that are not explained by the model!
Justified: The coding scheme must be justified by the model and the verbalization theory. One should not introduce new elements or concepts in the coding scheme that do not follow directly from the psychological model and the verbalization theory.
Grain size: Either the grain size must correspond to that of segments or it must be possible to objectively aggregate episodes that correspond to the categories in the coding scheme (else aggregation becomes part of coding which complicates the analysis). In the latter case aggregation should be done in a separate pass through the data. See also Section 7.5.2.
Unambiguous: The coding scheme must be clear enough to be used by outsiders. This is necessary to maintain objectivity of the coding procedure. Different coders must assign corresponding codes. We give a measure for this below.
Context independent: If a coding category describes a single cognitive process then it must be possible to recognize this without the context in which it appears. This is particularly important if we want to test the sequence predicted by the model. If the context in which a segment or episode appears is necessary to assign a code to it, it is no longer possible to really test the order because the order was used to assign the codes!

As with all methodological requirements, it is usually not possible to meet them for 100 per cent nor is it possible to construct an adequate coding scheme in one pass. The coding scheme (and the coding procedure) must be tested and evaluated on pilot protocols before it is applied to the actual data. For some criteria it is possible to quantify the extent to which they are met.

7.5 Coding procedures

7.5.1 Introduction

Coding means assigning labels to protocol episodes following the coding scheme. The result of applying the coding scheme to a protocol (raw data) will be a *coded protocol*. Segments or episodes that cannot be coded and sequences that are not predicted by the model but that do appear in the protocol reflect deviations of the model.

7.5.2 Aggregation

Transcription and segmentation are standard procedures that can be performed without any knowledge about the task or the model. This is not true of *aggregation*. Aggregation means collecting segments into groups that correspond in 'grain size' to the model. This is necessary if the model cannot describe protocols at the grain size of segments. For example, a model may contain a component 'compute the average' that is not elaborated further. In the protocol several segments together may correspond to this process. In this case only an episode, a sequence of segments can be recognized. Strictly speaking, aggregation of segments into episodes is part of the coding process because it requires knowledge about the model and cannot be performed in a model-independent way.

7.5.3 Coding

If possible, it is best to leave the coding of the protocols to independent coders. The researcher who has constructed the model and the coding scheme usually is too much attached to a certain research hypothesis to do the coding with an objective mind. Try to find coders who are not involved in the research project, and who have no specific interest in the outcome of the protocol analysis. This gives the best guarantee for objective (reproducible) coding. Give the coders only the minimal information about the purpose of the study and instruct them to be as precise as possible. Coders need to be trained in the use of the coding scheme. The protocols used for revising the coding scheme might be used for this.

The interpretation of a single phrase may be influenced by the context in which it appears. Take for example a subject who has been making a lot of errors and was very confused about the right way of solving the assigned word problem. If this subject would then say: 'the answer is 15', one would be inclined to interpret this step in the problem-solving as another wild guess. If the subject was someone who methodically followed a straightforward procedure, one would think it was just the outcome of the problem-solving process and thus the phrase 'the answer is 15' would be coded accordingly.

Measures one could take are: give coders only the minimal context information for coding. To refrain coders from using the context in which a protocol episode appears which might bias their coding - minimize the available context. The context involves:

(a) The subject who produced the protocol: shuffle protocols of different subjects and distribute them at random over coders.
(b) The content of the protocol: if possible cut the protocol in pieces that are just big enough to be coded reliably and shuffle these pieces. This will minimize the bias due to the context in which the fragment appears in the protocol. This is not always possible, sometimes protocol statements get unintelligible when lifted out of their contexts. In that case one must accept context-dependent coding.

7.5.4 Rating protocols or protocol fragments

If the model and the theory about the process are not procedural but structural, describing properties of protocols or protocol fragments, then protocols are rated. In this case scales are defined describing properties of the protocol and these are applied by coders following a procedure that is analogous to that for procedural models. In this case, the rating procedure produces standard numerical data and standard procedures for analysis can be applied.

7.6 Intercoder reliability

Before it is applied, a coding scheme and the coding procedure must be evaluated. In particular, correspondence between codes assigned by different coders to the same data must be found. If this correspondence, intercoder reliability, is low, then this means that the coding scheme is ambiguous. How can this correspondence be quantified? The techniques for quantifying correspondence all use one set of data that is coded by two (or sometimes more) coders. In the case of think aloud protocols, the data consist of an entire protocol, several protocols or one or more fragments. Intercoder reliability may vary over protocols and fragments so it is important to use a representative sample of the total set of protocols.

Reliability is usually quantified over segmented protocols. The segmentation itself is usually rather reliable and coding reliability can simply not be quantified over protocols that are segmented in different ways. It is also better to exclude irrelevant parts of the protocol (for example comments on the situation, reading fragments of text) because these inflate the reliability with respect to the actual cognitive process.

The selected data are then coded following the coding scheme that was designed in advance. Usually this means that they are assigned to a coding category. From these codings a cross-table can be constructed. Each cell contains the number of elements (for example fragments) as coded by both coders.

Take, for example, a small protocol which consists of eight segments. Two coders have coded this protocol. The coding scheme has only two categories: A and B. The two coders have coded the protocol as follows:

Segment	Code by coder 1	Code by coder 2	Correspondence
line 1	A	A	yes
line 2	A	B	no
line 3	B	B	yes
line 4	A	A	yes
line 5	A	A	yes
line 6	A	B	no
line 7	A	A	yes
line 8	A	A	yes

In this example both coders coded a line 5 times as A (line 1, 4, 5, 7 and 8), 1 time as B (line 3), and 2 times coder 2 assigned a B where coder 1 coded an A (line 2 and 6):

C1	C2	Frequency
A	A	5
A	B	2
B	A	0
B	B	1

From this coding the following cross-table is constructed:

Code	A	B	Total
A	5	2	7
B	0	1	1
Total	5	3	8

Correspondence between coders is now quantified as the association between their codings. The first obvious measure is the proportion of corresponding codes with respect to all codes. For the above table that would be the sum of the number of codes on the diagonal, namely 6 (5 + 1) divided by the total number, namely 8. This gives 75 per cent correspondence.

A conceptual problem is, though, that this measure is sensitive to differences in marginal frequencies, the proportion of the different coding categories used by the coders. In this example, code A is much more often used than code B, namely seven times by coder 1 and five times by coder 2, where B is used one time by coder 1 and three times by coder 2. This means that the expectation for an arbitrary segment to be coded as A, is higher than the expectation for it to be coded as B. In this small example the need for correction for marginal frequencies might not be so obvious. But take for example a protocol of 100 segments. If 99 segments are coded as A by both coders and only 1 segment is coded as B by one of the coders, the correspondence would be 99 per cent. However, it is not fair to say that in this case an extremely high intercoder reliability has been reached. For a segment to be coded as A, the chance was 99 per cent. So in some sense the coders did not do better than if the coding had been done by a random generator. The one segment about which there was no agreement between coders is far more significant than all the other segments which were coded the same.

In another example, where from the 100 segments 50 were coded as A by both coders, and 49 as B, a reliability of 99 per cent indicates much more correspondence between the coders. In this case every segment had a chance of some 50 per cent to be coded as A. In this case the fact that the coders coded nearly all segments the same, cannot be ascribed to chance.

Several measures have been invented that to some extent correct for differences in marginal frequencies. These measures show subtle differences in behaviour and in the underlying notion of association. One frequently used measure, that we recommend, is Kappa. This measure is based on a correction for marginal frequencies and defines association as the relative proportion of corresponding codes with the following correction:

$$\text{Kappa} = \frac{(\text{proportion corresponding} - \text{expected proportion corresponding})}{(1 - \text{expected proportion corresponding})}$$

Here the expected proportion corresponding is calculated by multiplying and adding marginal frequencies. In the example the correspondence for A that can be expected from the marginal frequencies of B is $7/8 \times 5/8 = 0.55$. For B we will get $1/8 \times 3/8 = 0.05$ and then the total is $0.55 + 0.05 = 0.60$. For the table above Kappa is:

$$\text{Kappa} = \frac{(0.75 - 0.60)}{(1 - 0.60)} = \frac{0.15}{0.40} = 0.38$$

So, in this example we have gone from a proportion of corresponding codings of 0.75, to a Kappa of 0.38. The fact that Kappa is lower is due to the fact that code A is more frequently used than B. That the difference is so great is due to the fact that this example is so very small.

What will happen to the two extreme examples of the 100 segments protocol if we calculate the Kappa? In the case of 99 segments coded as A the Kappa is:

$$\text{Kappa} = \frac{(0.99 - 0.99)}{(1 - 0.99)} = 0.00$$

In the example of 50 segments coded as A and 49 segments coded as B by both coders the Kappa is:

$$\text{Kappa} = \frac{(0.99 - 0.499)}{(1 - 0.499)} = 0.98$$

The Kappa makes a correction for the correspondence that can be expected from the marginal frequencies. This is a conservative estimate of intercoder reliability because similar marginal frequencies will make Kappa low where one could argue that similar marginal frequencies themselves indicate intercoder reliability. Since the proportion correspondence is an optimistic estimate it is best to report both proportion correspondence and Kappa.

Let us now look at a larger example. A set of 98 segments is coded by two coders: Coder 1 and Coder 2. The coding scheme has 5 categories and the table below shows how many fragments were scored as A by both, as A by Coder 1 and B by Coder 2, etc.

Code	A	B	C	D	E	Total
A	6	0	2	0	0	8
B	1	48	11	0	0	60
C	1	2	17	0	0	20
D	0	0	0	5	3	8
E	0	0	0	0	2	2
Total	8	50	30	5	5	98

The proportion corresponding codes with respect to all codes is calculated by dividing the sum of the number of codes on the diagonal (81) by the total number (98). This gives 83 per cent correspondence.

Now we calculate Kappa. The expected proportion corresponding is calculated by multiplying and adding marginal frequencies. For example the correspondence for A that can be expected from the marginal frequencies of B is: $8/98 \times 8/98 = 0.007$

The expected proportion corresponding values are:

Code	Marginal frequencies		Expected proportion corresponding
A	8/98 × 8/98	=	0.007
B	50/98 × 60/98	=	0.312
C	30/98 × 20/98	=	0.062
D	5/98 × 8/98	=	0.004
E	5/98 × 2/98	=	0.001
Total			0.386

For the table above Kappa is:

$$\text{Kappa} = \frac{(0.83 - 0.386)}{(1 - 0.386)} = \frac{0.444}{0.614} = 0.72$$

As we see in this example, there is a difference in the outcome of the two measures (0.83 versus 0.72), but the difference is not as large as in the previous example (0.75 versus 0.38). Of course it is hard to say when the Kappa is sufficiently high. We would, generally speaking, say a Kappa should be above 0.70 in order to have an intercoder reliability that is acceptable. If the Kappa is less, we would strongly advise to improve the coding scheme.

7.7 Comparing the coded protocols with the models

7.7.1 Introduction

We now will discuss the stage of protocol analysis that is crucial in the hypothesis testing style, i.e. comparing the coded protocols with the model. If the model is stated in terms of properties of protocols rather than procedures, these properties are measured by counting items or by rating protocols. This requires procedures that are standard in social science research. Comparing *procedural* models with protocols involves a different notion of fit that we shall discuss here.

7.7.2 Comparing protocols with procedural models

Each segment in each of the protocols should fit within the model. In general a model predicts more than one possible process (we called this non-deterministic models). Each of these corresponds to a possible coded protocol and fitting means verifying if the coded protocol is one of the predicted protocols. You look at the coded segments one by one and compare them with the predicted steps of the model. If a segment (or episode) does not fit into the model because it cannot be generated from the model and the state of the reasoning process then this is marked as a deviation. These deviations are counted. Differences between the coded protocols and the predictions from a process model, may be of three kinds:

1. The protocols show processes which are not predicted by the model.
2. The model predicts processes not shown by the protocols.
3. The protocols show processes in a different sequence than predicted by the model.

1. Unpredicted processes: Unpredicted processes occur when there are segments or fragments in the protocol which cannot be coded, not even under the category 'not task-related or meta-statements'. This means that there is no category in the model for the verbalized actions. For example, in the exploratory phase of Hamel's study, he encountered remarks on the assignment related to how the building should look. These kinds of processes were not at first part of the model and thus were not represented in the coding scheme. What should you decide about your model if you have one or more uncodable segments? The simplest judgement is that your model is false. If the model is detailed and makes strong predictions instead of allowing many possibilities then it is likely to be false. However, usually an interesting question is to what extent the model is false. How much behaviour is covered correctly by the model? Generally speaking, one could say that the more uncoded segments are found, the more evidence there is against the model. This analysis must be done for each element of the model to show which elements are responsible for the discrepancies. Such discrepancies are especially of interest when there are unpredicted processes in protocols from different subjects, and even more so when there exists correspondence between those subjects on the unpredicted processes.

2. Absence of predicted processes: A similar argument applies to the absence of processes that were predicted by the model. If the absence cannot be explained by the verbalization model (as a verbalization failure) then it contradicts the model. The best measure for the absence of predicted processes is simply their number or proportion of the total number of predicted processes.

3. Unpredicted sequences: Sometimes a protocol shows the predicted categories but in a sequence that is not predicted by the model. This applies to process models that contain predictions about sequences of events. Here again unpredicted sequences are evidence against the model and it is necessary to quantify the difference. One method is to take *transitions* as a unit of analysis instead of reasoning steps. A process model may predict possible transitions and unpredicted transitions can simply be counted. This method was used in Hamel's study. In 12 protocols a total of 2829 transitions occurred, 2818 of which were conform the model. Hamel could argue that the remaining deviations were not of such nature that his model should be rejected. Transitions do not take the wider context into account: whether a transition is possible depends on the previous transition and not on any wider context.

A process model usually specifies component processes and a relation between these components. For example, a model that predicts the processes *orientation, execution* and *evaluation* can also specify sub-processes of these three. It can now specify that these processes will occur in this order. This means that sequences are predicted at two levels of detail. This gives the same types of errors as we discussed (missing and unpredicted elements and unpredicted sequences) but at different levels. This complicates the analysis. We have no real solution for this problem. A simple method is to report results for each (important) level separately.

7.7.3 Issues in quantifying the fit

There are several issues that complicate quantifying the fit between protocol and model. These are:

(a) Degrees of freedom in the model: A model may not specify a unique description of a protocol, but it may allow several possibilities. These may in turn be dependent on events that occur during problem-solving. For instance, if the subject makes an unpredicted mistake, problem-solving may follow an unpredicted course, but still fit the model. A model allowing many different behaviours is of course weaker, in the sense that it has less predictive power than one that predicts fewer possibilities.

(b) Differences in size of the protocols: Two protocols may differ in length not because of differences in thought processes, but because of different styles of verbalization. This may affect the coding. Usually this effect is reduced by aggregation, because a protocol that is more verbose than another because of the verbalization process, is likely to be the same if phrases are aggregated to problem-solving episodes. If phrases are used then a standardization on the size of the protocol (by using the percentages) is a good solution.

7.7.4 Comparing sets of protocols

Sometimes groups of protocols are compared, for example sets of protocols of two types of subjects in a psychological experiment or of subjects before and after an experimental treatment. If dimensions are used and protocols can be assigned a score on a dimension, possibly aggregating process properties, then the situation is the same as in standard experiments and the same analysis procedures apply. For example, one may count the proportion (or number) of *orientation* fragments in protocols of novices and experts.

A special problem occurs if the comparison involves process structures. Suppose that we compare beginners and experts in architectural design and predict that experts will follow the order *orientation - execute - evaluate* where beginners will mix the order. How can we quantify the difference between a set of (coded) beginners protocols and a set of (coded) expert protocols? A possibility is to calculate the rank correlation between each protocol and the expert sequence and test the difference between the two groups. However, this procedure suffers from the effect of different numbers of protocol fragments (beginners are likely to need more reasoning to solve the problems than experts). Ideally this effect should disappear when a good coding scheme is used because different ways to verbalize a cognitive process will result in the same code being assigned to a protocol fragment (even if the fragment is longer in one protocol than in another). However, in practice this is not always adequate. The solution followed in practice is to define properties that abstract from these levels on an ad hoc basis.

7.8 Computer support tools for analysis

7.8.1 Introduction

Transcribing and coding or annotating protocols is a very time-consuming activity. Currently, several types of computer systems are being developed to support this task. These systems are still in a stage of development and exploration and they are not yet standardized or easily accessible. Therefore we only summarize the principles of these systems to give an impression of tools that are likely to be available in the near future.

7.8.2 Indexing tools

One useful type of tools are systems that can index and retrieve pieces of text. If protocols are transcribed and stored in the computer, fragments of the text can be marked and given an index. These indexes can again be stored. For example, we can give each fragment an individual reference but collect all references of fragments where the protocol concerns, for example, 'selecting a schema'. This makes it possible to quickly retrieve all fragments where this occurs. This type of tool is relatively easy to build. It can be constructed using most hypertext and database systems. The structure of the database is to use segments or aggregated fragments of the written text as entries in the database and to index these by coding category, coder, date (of collecting the protocol), problem (that is the problem solved here) and subject. Future technical developments will make it possible to store the spoken protocol and index it in this way, thus avoiding transcription and keeping additional information in the spoken protocol.

7.8.3 An implemented model as tool

The most powerful tools are those that correspond to implemented psychological models that can be used to recognize uncoded or coded protocols. The model of physics problem-solving described in Chapter 8 has been implemented. The resulting system can actually solve most of the problems that were used in the study described there. A recognition mode was added to this system as follows. In recognition mode, the system is given the problem and then it asks the user of the system (who has the protocol), what the next lines in the protocol are. The answer must be given in a predefined form. The system then checks if this is consistent with what it expects. If this is the case, it continues. If the protocol deviates from the expected solution path, this is noted as an *unpredicted* step (which violates the model). In many cases the system can understand the step taken in the protocol and resume problem-solving from the new situation. In this way protocols can be coded quickly and an overview of unpredicted and missing events can be produced automatically.

7.9 Reporting the results of protocol analysis

Analysis of think aloud protocols usually leads to a large amount of documentation: the typed protocols, the detailed model, the coded protocols, the comparison between the model and the coded protocols. Technical reports on studies using protocol analysis are, generally speaking, large ones. In order to justify the conclusions drawn from such a study, every step taken in the process of analysis must be explained and reasons for decisions made, must be given. For example, if you decide to leave out certain fragments of a protocol, you must provide evidence that these fragments do not falsify the model. If you want to draw the firm conclusion from your study that experts put much more effort into orientation processes than novices, you have to show which protocol fragments are considered as verbalizations of orientation processes for every subject under study. In order to enable other researchers to verify your findings and conclusions, a lot of information must be provided. This is already a problem for technical reports and even more so for an article. There is no full agreement on the way in which the results of protocol analysis should be reported in scientific articles. Here we give a proposal that tries to balance the degree to which an independent researcher can reproduce the result of the analysis and the space restrictions imposed by most journals. Next to the usual description of the research question, the subjects, the task and the experimental procedure, the following items should be described:

Short fragment of a verbatim protocol: This fragment gives the reader an impression of the kinds of processes and verbalizations used by the subjects. If possible, present a fragment where the subject is working on an easily understandable task, so that the fragment is clear to the reader who is not a task expert. If the fragment is not self-evident, explain shortly what the subject is doing.

Schematic description of the model: If the description of the model does not take up too much space, one can include the description of the entire model. However, if the model is elaborate, is very detailed or has several layers, a summary should be given. A schematic figure, accompanied by a short description, is a good way of presenting a model, providing an insightful overview. You should indicate shortly how the model is extended in its full form. Sometimes it is useful to present some parts of the detailed model, for example the full decomposition of one main category.

The main categories of the coding scheme: If the coding scheme is concise, give the complete coding scheme, otherwise list the main categories. For one category, the complete coding should be given. State shortly how the coding scheme is derived from the model. Give some examples of how the categories are reflected in the protocols. For example: 'category orientation: remarks about related problems'.

Outcomes of the coding in an aggregated manner: Present the main findings of the coding in a concise manner, for example in a table with the coding frequencies on the main categories.

Intercoder reliability of the coding: Explain how intercoder reliability was determined and present the outcome, usually both the reliability figure and the Kappa. Give the number of coders, describe who they were, and the percentage of the verbalizations on which the reliability-score was based. If the reliability is not very high, give an explanation, if available.

Fit between the model and the coded protocols: Discuss how the coded protocols are related to the model, give arguments and examples. If possible, provide a quantitative measure of the fit. These should be reported per element of the model (that is, per coding category).

An example of a fully worked out analysis of a protocol fragment: Present a short fragment of a protocol, say how it was coded and how it compares to the model.

Literature

A discussion of association measures is given in, for example, Everitt (1977).

Chapter 8

Examples

8.1 Introduction

In this chapter we present examples of the use of the think aloud method to illustrate different styles of modelling and coding. The first and second examples concern psychological studies of problem-solving in physics and computer programming. The third illustrates the use of the think aloud method in knowledge acquisition in medical diagnosis.

8.2 Solving physics problems

8.2.1 Introduction

To illustrate the use of protocol analysis we present an example borrowed from Jansweijer (1988). The main purpose of this study is to develop a theory about *problem-solving* in so-called 'semantically rich domains'. By semantically rich domains Jansweijer means domains in which a diversity of knowledge is needed to solve problems and in which the problems are often ill defined. As domain for his study he chose thermodynamics, a topic in physics. The focus of the study was on differences between novice and advanced problem solvers. The main hypothesis, derived from previous research in education and psychology, was that an important difference between novices and advanced problem solvers is in the method that they follow. Advanced problem solvers pay more attention to analysis of the problem. This process is called *orientation* in psychology. This enables them to select appropriate knowledge to apply to a problem. Novices tend to skip the orientation and look for a formula that can be used to calculate what is asked in the problem. If that formula needs more information, they simply look for additional formulae until a set of equations is found that can be solved for the asked.

Jansweijer developed a computational model of advanced problem-solving that could solve a large part of the problems (if they were presented to the system in a structured form). First we will give the text of an example problem, the advanced level model and then the coding of a protocol. Finally we present Jansweijer's conclusions based on the comparison of a series of protocols of one subject with the advanced model.

8.2.2 An example problem

Here follows the text of one of the 35 thermodynamic problems Jansweijer used:

An isolated container with a content of 800 dm^3 oxygen, is rapidly brought from a starting pressure of 120 kilopascals to 170 kilopascals, so no warmth is exchanged with the environment. How much is the new volume?

The problem is about a quick expansion of gas, without exchange of heat with the environment. This makes the assumption that the process is adiabatic plausible. For adiabatic processes Poisson's law ($P \times V^\gamma = constant$) is applicable. In a format which relates the begin state to the end state this formula reads:

$$P_1 \times V_1^\gamma = P_2 \times V_2^\gamma$$

P_1, P_2 and V_1 are given, while V_2 is the quantity asked for.

So: $V_2^\gamma = \frac{P_1}{P_2} \times V_1^\gamma$ and $V_2 = \sqrt[\gamma]{\frac{P_1}{P_2} \times V_1^\gamma}$

which can be filled in and computed.

8.2.3 The model of advanced problem solving

The solution above is the result of task analysis. It was obtained by consulting experts (in this case physics teachers and on previous research on solution methods for physics problems). Jansweijer starts from the assumption that all problem-solving behaviour of a subject is determined by the knowledge the subject has concerning the task at hand. The difference between novices and experts is thus not attributed to differences in the cognitive mechanisms but to differences in knowledge. Therefore the model concerns the knowledge needed to solve these problems. Two main types of knowledge are distinguished: knowledge about physics concepts, principles and formulae and knowledge about problem-solving. Here we focus on the knowledge about problem-solving. Jansweijer based this part of the model on the general problem-solving theory which distinguishes three main processes: *orientate*, *solve* and *evaluate*. Within those processes different sub-processes are distinguished. For the orientation processes, these are: READ_PROBLEM, SKETCH and SCHEMATIZE. This leads to the following decomposition:

```
ORIENTATE
    READ_PROBLEM
        READ_GLOBAL
        EXTRACT_FEATURES
    SKETCH
        READ_FRAGMENT
        EXTRACT_FEATURES
        CANONIZE
        CONSTRUCT_PROBLEM_SKETCH
    SCHEMATIZE
        DETERMINE_SYSTEM
        DETERMINE_STATES
        DETERMINE_PROCESS
        ANALYSE_ASKED
        ANALYSE_QUALITATIVE
```

READ_PROBLEM means the reading of the problem text as a task consisting of: read globally (READ_GLOBAL) and notice keywords like 'adiabatic', 'quick' and 'dynamic' (EXTRACT_FEATURES). In the example problem, the expression 'is rapidly brought from a starting pressure of 120 kilopascals to 170 kilopascals, so no warmth is exchanged' indicates an 'adiabatic' thermodynamic process.

SKETCH is described in the model as a task at which the text is read carefully sentence by sentence (READ_FRAGMENT). The other sub-tasks are again noticing keywords (EXTRACT_FEATURES) and the reduction of non-standard devices to their standard form (CANONIZE). The EXTRACT_FEATURES task listed here is the same as listed under READ_PROBLEM above. The model states that EXTRACT_FEATURES either takes place while reading the problem, or under SKETCH. The last sub-task under SKETCH concerns the structuring of all the givens into a knowledge structure (CONSTRUCT_PROBLEM_SKETCH).

In the example problem this means that a representation of the problem is made that includes the two states and the properties of these states.
SCHEMATIZE is subdivided into five sub-tasks. DETERMINE_SYSTEM chooses the thermodynamical system. DETERMINE_STATES decides on the basis of the givens how many states there are and tries to detect the state variables that together describe the states. DETERMINE_PROCESS analyses the changes that are described in the problem text. It aims at connecting the detected states by state changes. ANALYSE_ASKED determines the type of unknown: is it a state variable or a process variable? ANALYSE_QUALITATIVE has as its task to make a qualitative judgment on what kind of process is taking place and what kind of changes are occurring (their direction and estimated size).

After this orientation process the model gets into the solving process. Its decomposition is as follows:

```
SOLVE
    SOLVE_FOR_VARIABLE
        CLASSIFY_VARIABLES
        RESOLVE_VARIABLE
            GENERALIZE_VARIABLES
            SELECT_PRINCIPLE
            CHECK_APPLICABILITY
            SPECIFY_EQUATION
            SIMPLIFY_EQUATION

    COMPUTE
        SUBSTITUTE_EQUATIONS
        FILL_EQUATIONS
        CALCULATE
```

SOLVE_FOR_VARIABLE generates a system of equations that is solvable for the asked. This is realized by the sub-tasks CLASSIFY_VARIABLES and RESOLVE_VARIABLE.
CLASSIFY_VARIABLES looks if there are still unknowns left (variables that are neither known, nor calculable, nor retrievable). If there are no unknowns left, then there is apparently a solvable system of equations. If there are still unknowns left, then CLASSIFY_VARIABLE repeatedly chooses one unknown, for which the task RESOLVE_VARIABLE is performed.

RESOLVE_VARIABLE has five sub-tasks. GENERALIZE_VARIABLES determines what kind of variables are under concern (what physics concepts). That means finding out what the dimensions of the givens are and what the dimension of the asked is. By dimensions concepts like mass, temperature, pressure and volume are meant. Subsequently SELECT_PRINCIPLE preselects potentially applicable physics principles. This concerns principles that relate the dimensions of the givens to the dimension of the asked. In case there are more than one applicable principles, the one that introduces the least unknown variables is chosen. CHECK_APPLICABILITY then checks if all conditions for the application of the chosen principle are fulfilled. SPECIFY_EQUATION derives from the general physics principle the specific equation that relates the quantities stated in the problem at hand. SIMPLIFY_EQUATION finally simplifies the generated equation. It eliminates those variables from the equation that cannot be quantified because they are expressed in terms of one another.
COMPUTE has three sub-tasks. SUBSTITUTE_EQUATION substitutes the subsequent series of equations until the asked is found on the left-hand side and the right-hand side shows only knowns. FILL_EQUATION substitutes the symbols at the right hand side with their numerical values. CALCULATE calculates the asked from this final equation.

Finally the problem-solving process ends with the evaluation phase.

EVALUATE
    CHECK_SOLUTION

The model proposes that the solution is checked.
    This description gives only the level of the problem solving method and not the physics knowledge. The actual model gives detailed predictions of the intermediate results and reasoning steps.

8.2.4 Design of the experiments

Before think aloud protocols can be collected, subjects and problems must be selected. To make the results as relevant as possible for the normal situation, subjects were university students. The novice subjects were psychology students who had done some elementary physics in secondary school. They were selected on the basis of a pilot study in which they solved mechanics problems while thinking aloud. Many subjects in this pilot study could solve hardly any of the mechanics problems. As novices those subjects were selected that showed some initial competence in solving mechanics problems. The advanced subjects were physics students who were rated as very good by their teachers. Half of these subjects had also been trained in a problem-solving method for physics problems. The problems were selected from exercises in a textbook on thermodynamics. The problems varied considerably in difficulty. The simple problems can be solved by most novices after reading the introductory text and the most difficult ones are hard even for the advanced subjects. The example problem above is one of the easier problems. Due to the amount of work, the protocols of only 6 subjects were used. They solved 35 problems. Because the computational model could solve 17 of the problems, the analysis was limited to those. All subjects solved the same problems. Next the model of the advanced problem solvers was compared with the protocols of novices and advanced problem solvers. The prediction was that at the level of the problem-solving method, the model would fit the protocols of the advanced subjects much better than the protocols of the novices.

8.2.5 A protocol

We illustrate the analysis of the protocols with a protocol of an advanced problem-solver for the above problem.

```
1:  an isolated container with a content
2:  of eight hundred cubic decimetres
3:  containing oxygen, is rapidly brought
4:  from a starting pressure
5:  of hundred-and-twenty kilopascal
6:  to hundred-and-seventy kilopascal,
7:  so no warmth
8:  is exchanged with the environment
9:  how much is the new volume?
10: v1,
11: that's ... eight hundred ten to the power
12: minus three
13: [writes down:  V₁ = 800 × 10⁻³]
14: [writes down:  P₁ = 1.2 × 10⁵]
15: t1 is t1 [writes down:  T₁ = T₁]
16: that goes to v2 p2 t2,
17: [writes down:  V₂ = ... P₂ = ... T₂ = ...]
18: in which t2 is also unknown
19: [writes down:  T₂ = T₂]
20: one comma seven ten to the power five
```

(Line 13: $V_1 = 800 \times 10^{-3}$; Line 14: $P_1 = 1.2 \times 10^5$; Line 15: $T_1 = T_1$; Line 17: $V_2 = \ldots P_2 = \ldots T_2 = \ldots$; Line 19: $T_2 = T_2$)

Examples

21: [writes down: $P_2 = 1.7 \times 10^5$]
22: the volume is asked for [writes down: $V_2 = ?$]
23: adiabatic,
24: so now just ... p times v to the power
25: gamma is constant ... p1 v1 gamma
26: is p2 v2 gamma
27: [writes down: $P_1 \times V_1^\gamma = P_2 \times V_2^\gamma$]
28: v2 to the power gamma is p1 v1 to the power gamma
29: divided by p2
30: [writes down: $V_2^\gamma = \frac{P_1}{P_2} \times V_1^\gamma$] v2 to the power gamma which
31: is then ... oxygen
32: just calculate gamma,
33: two point nine
34: this times four, I reckoned yes,
35: is one comma four
36: [writes down: $\gamma = 1.4$] so then v2 to the power gamma
37: is ... p1 one comma two ten to the power
38: five,
39: divided by ... one comma seven ten
40: to the power five,
41: cross out,
42: times v1,
43: zero comma eight to the ... one comma
44: four
45: [writes down: $V_2^\gamma = \frac{1.2 \times 10^5}{1.7 \times 10^5} \times 0.8^\gamma$]
46: cancels 10^5 out]
47: thus v2 that is then ... er
48: one comma four becomes already
49: from this total thing
50: from one comma two divided by one
51: comma seven times comma eight to the
52: ... one comma four.
53: [writes down: $V_2 = \sqrt[1.4]{\frac{1.2}{1.7} \times 0.8^{1.4}}$]
54: eeer ... point eight ...
55: [uses calculator] to the power
56: that is ... times two ... divided
57: by one point seven that is,
58: one comma four reversed to the ...
59: just store store zero

```
60: eeer yes,
61: I do not know whether store one,
62: recall one to the  ...   ehm  ...   recall
63: zero to the  ...   yes,
64: nothing,
65: recall one is  ...   ehm
66: v2 is zero comma sixty two,
67: cubic metres
68: [writes down:   = 0.62m³]
69: pressure is increased,
70: volume decreases, yes ...
```

8.2.6 Coding the protocol

In this study no separate coding schema was used. The model was precise, detailed and close enough to potential verbalizations to be used as coding schema as well. Here we code the protocol in terms of the model noting possible discrepancies. Note that the model consists of layers. Only the most specific layers correspond directly to protocol segments. For example, the process ORIENTATE consists of several sub-processes. Only the most specific sub-processes (READ_GLOBAL, DETERMINE_STATES, DETERMINE_PROCESS, DETERMINE_STATES, ANALYSE_ASKED, ANALYSE_QUALITATIVE) appear in the protocols. Also note that the description above is for the general case. For some problems sub-processes may not be relevant. For example, the process SIMPLIFY_EQUATION will only take place if an equation can actually be simplified. The more detailed version of the model (in particular the computational model) is able to make these detailed predictions. Below we shall not analyse the protocol at that level of detail but focus on the problem solving method.

Lines:	Model elements:	Comments:
	ORIENTATE	
	READ_PROBLEM	
1-9	READ_GLOBAL	OK
		At this point the model predicts EXTRACT_FEATURES. This does not appear in the protocol.

Examples

	SCHEMATIZE	Next the model predicts a series of steps for SKETCH. However, this subject directly proceeds with SCHEMATIZE.
		Here the process DETERMINE_SYSTEM is missing.
10-15	DETERMINE_STATES	OK
16	DETERMINE_PROCESS	OK
17-21	DETERMINE_STATES	OK
22	ANALYSE_ASKED	OK
23	ANALYSE_QUALITATIVE	OK
		SCHEMATIZE is as predicted.
	SOLVE	
	SOLVE_FOR_VARIABLE	
		The process CLASSIFY_VARIABLES is not predicted for the current problem.
	RESOLVE_VARIABLE	
		Here the process GENERALIZE_VARIABLES is missing.
24-25	SELECT_PRINCIPLE	OK
		Here the process CHECK_APPLICABILITY is missing.
26-27	SPECIFY_EQUATION	OK
		The process SIMPLIFY_EQUATION is not predicted here.
	COMPUTE	
28-30	SUBSTITUTE_EQUATIONS	OK
31-54	FILL_EQUATIONS	OK
55-68	CALCULATE	OK
	EVALUATE	
69-70	CHECK_SOLUTION	OK

As the reader can see, all statements in the protocol are predicted by the model. Some processes do not appear here because they are not predicted by the more detailed version of the model. These are: CANONIZE, CLASSIFY_VARIABLES and SIMPLIFY_EQUATION. However, several predicted processes are missing and these are potential discrepancies with the model:

EXTRACT_FEATURES: It is possible that the subject selected the formula without explicitly extracting the feature 'adiabatic'. There is no good reason (such as automated process) to assume that this was done very quickly so we have to assume that it was skipped.
SKETCH with its sub-processes: the subject constructs a schema (in physics terms) without first constructing a sketch. For this problem sketch and schema are very similar so this is easy to do. It is not consistent with the model, though.
DETERMINE_SYSTEM: This is not mentioned but it is very plausible that this was automated. In this case the selection of the thermodynamic system is trivial (the gas in the container). This will not be verbalized here.
GENERALIZE_VARIABLES: This is also trivial in this case and the fact that it does not appear in the protocol can be attributed to automation.
CHECK_APPLICABILITY: This is skipped. Because the subject also did not perform EXTRACT_FEATURES (which is a cue for applicability) it is quite possible that did process did not take place. A missing process.

This means that all of the 70 protocol segments are predicted by the model but that 3 processes remain missing from the protocol.

8.2.7 Results

The model was compared with the protocols of two novice and four advanced problem solvers. The model is tested on three levels:

1. Validation of the sequence of tasks within the model.
2. Validation of the completeness of the model (are there protocol fragments that cannot be coded in terms of the model?).
3. Validation of the level of detail and correctness of the model (are there model statements that are never found in the protocols?).

8.2.8 The sequence of tasks

The task structure specified in the model largely agreed with the task structures found in the protocols of the subject. In all protocols the orientation task is carried out completely before the actual solving of the problem. Therefore the model provides an accurate picture of the analysis of the problem text that takes place before the solving of the problem. Diversions are not found at the global level of the task structure but within sub-tasks. For example, the sequence of steps within SCHEMATIZE does not always agree with the sequence the model predicts. Jansweijer concludes that his model is more in line with the problem-solving behaviour of advanced subjects than models proposed by some other researchers that do not take an orientation phase into account.

There was a clear difference between the protocols of the advanced problem solvers and the novices. The clearest difference was in the ORIENTATION process. Novice protocols show less ORIENTATION and also this process does not take place where it is predicted but is spread out between other processes.

8.2.9 The completeness of the model

The model is not complete. This follows from the fact that 17 per cent of all protocol statements of this subject was coded as **NO MATCH**, which means that no parallel action could be found in the model. In many protocols, for example, those **NO MATCH** statements concern 'recognition of the problem as a particular problem type'. Statements were made, like:

```
'is just like the previous problem, you can just say ...'
'this is a ... well, rather a standard problem'
```

Jansweijer concludes that the model would increase in completeness if a component for the recognition of problem types were added. Another kind of incompleteness detected concerned the derivation of a physics principle. The advanced subject consequently starts from the most general, basic principle, whereas the model in most cases initially chooses an more specific principle. And finally, the model lacks the ability to consider its own problem-solving process, where the subject provides evidence that he does have this ability:

```
' ... well yes, I do not need to further what you call it, with
the components, that makes no difference, anyhow'
'and that is ... well, it should in any case be larger'
```

8.2.10 The level of detail of the model

At some points the level of detail of the model is found to be too high. For example, within SKETCH the model has separate tasks for reading the problem text sentence by sentence, extracting the important features, integrating the givens in a sketch, finding the asked and determining the device in its standard form. The subject under investigation tends to integrate most of these tasks with the model's next task SCHEMATIZE. Jansweijer concludes that although the model is at some points too detailed this does hardly endanger its validity. He argues that it is very plausible that the separate tasks specified by the model are still carried out by the subject, but automated to such a degree that they no longer appear as separate statements in the protocols.

8.2.11 Conclusion

The example provided above shows how protocol analysis can be used to investigate a scientific question. In this case the evaluation of the model showed that the model was quite accurate. The analysis of the protocols formed an adequate basis for further refinement of the model.

8.3 Explaining novice errors in computer programming

8.3.1 Introduction

Several studies of computer programming have used the think aloud method. Most of these studies were aimed at understanding the errors and difficulties of novice computer programmers. One example is the study reported by van Someren (1990). Subjects solved programming exercises while thinking aloud. The analysis of the protocols was based on a detailed analysis of the programming problems and the hypothesis that errors were due to misleading analogies between constructions in the programming language that was used in the exercises and structures in our common language or in other programming languages.

8.3.2 The model

On the basis of this idea a psychological model of programming behaviour was constructed. This model is in the form of production rules that transform an algorithm into a Prolog program. The model does not address other cognitive processes that also play an important role in programming, such as: understanding the problem, verifying the program, finding bugs and repairing these. A particular student can be modelled as a subset of these implementation rules. Some rules ('malrules') are incorrect, producing incorrect programs. The malrules are based on analogy between structures in the original algorithm and in the Prolog programming language. To construct this model we started with a task analysis. How can a correct program be constructed from the initial problem specification? Consider the following example of an algorithm for computing the maximum of a list of numbers:

```
Maximum(List, Max):
  Initialize Max at 0
  REPEAT
    take next element N from list
    IF N > Max THEN ASSIGN N TO Max
  UNTIL list is EMPTY
```

There are several ways to implement this in Prolog. What is needed in any case is a condition to stop the running of the program when the end of the list is reached, in order to avoid an endless loop. The condition to stop the REPEAT cycle is that the list is empty. What is also needed in Prolog structures, is a variable to which the largest number found can be assigned, so that when the program stops running, it can give back this maximum.

Lists in Prolog consist of a 'head' and a 'tail'. The head is the first element of the list, the tail is the rest of the list. Take for example the list [2,7,8,4], the head is 2, the tail is [7,8,4]. A list can be empty, noted down as: [].

A Prolog program consists of a sequence of 'clauses'. There are two types of clauses. One type is a kind of IF-THEN rules and the other is a kind of facts. The program is started by calling it with a structure that has the same form as the THEN-part of one or more rules. So for example, the program for finding the maximum of the list [7, 8, 4] would be started by the call max([7, 8, 4], M) where the result would appear as the value for M. The stop-condition part can be implemented in Prolog, for example as one of the following 'fact' structures:

`max([], M, M).` or `max([M], M).`

depending on the rest of the program. However, there is a Prolog clause

`max([], M):- fail.`

that is wrong, although, it is actually more similar to the expression 'UNTIL list is EMPTY' than the correct implementations. The special Prolog construct `fail` has the effect of simply stopping the execution at this point, and the maximum number is not exported. The correct implementations have additional effects (passing on substitutions for the variable Max).

A Prolog structure that is also false, but perhaps superficially even more appropriate is:

`max([], M).`

Like the previous structure this is intended to implement an action that must be applied when the 'empty list' [] is encountered by the system. At that point the procedure must stop.

This example illustrates how implementation errors can be explained by naive analogies between the algorithm and the implementation. Reasoning steps in the protocol were matched with applications of rules (and malrules). No additional coding scheme was constructed because application of rules and malrules can be recognized both from the results of a reasoning step and from the protocol text. Coding was done at a fairly low level of granularity: episodes in the protocols were coded as showing clear evidence of applying a reasoning step from the novice model or not. The frequency with which rules and malrules match protocol fragments were reported. The results show that most rules and malrules appeared in the protocols, which gives some initial support to the model. Some rules did not appear in the protocols. The author has no good explanation for this, other than the relatively small set of data. In this study other support for the model is presented that is based on (false) programs that were constructed by students taking a course in Prolog. Many false programs can be explained from the application of malrules. This is an example of the use of several types of data to evaluate a model.

8.3.3 Design of the study

Subjects in this experiment were students who took an introductory course in Prolog programming. Two types of data were used: a collection of programs with errors that were produced by students during practical work and a set of think aloud protocols.

8.3.4 An analysed protocol

To illustrate the coding procedure we give a protocol fragment and the rules and malrules that were identified in this fragment.

Protocol + subject's notes	Analysis and comments
1: err, stop-condition must be the list is finished	This shows that the subject has implicitly already found an initial algorithm.
2: he has to look at the whole list, anyway,	Repeats algorithm.
3: because otherwise he can never know which is the biggest	
4: call the predicate 'biggest' for the moment	'Biggest' corresponds to the procedure that was called 'Max' in the description above.
5: and it can only say it when the first list is empty	
6: so the given list is an empty list	
7: so the final stop-condition,	
8: that has to come in another argument	
9: this is the variable for the biggest	This variable corresponds to the variable M in the description above.
10: anyway the stop-condition [writes: biggest([], X)]	Uses false implementation rule. The implementation is based on the algorithm described above: Initialize Max at 0 REPEAT take next element N from list IF N > Max THEN ASSIGN N TO Max UNTIL list is EMPTY
11: ... perhaps it will be 1 of 3	(he means: three clauses)
12: again a 'biggest', that is I have a list,	
13: a list with a head and a tail,	
14: you have to look at it number by number	
15: another biggest,	
16: that means that I have a list	
17: a list with head and tail	

18: you should look at it number
    by number
19: er, here I have another
    argument ...
20: and that is the biggest, er,
21: now I do it so that he takes
    the first,
22: fixes it
23: then looks at the head of   Here the body of the REPEAT
    the tail   loop is partially implemented
    [writes: biggest([H|T],Y):- following an incorrect
       compare(H,X,Y).]   implementation rule.
25: you have to fix that instead
    of the other
26: that is how it must be
27: and finally, er, if you have
    done them all
28: you can go to the stop-condition
29: that is the principle
30: which should work, I think   Explicitly evaluates the resulting
                                  program.

The resulting (erroneous) Prolog program is:

```
biggest([], X).
biggest([H|T], Y):-
   compare(H, X, Y).
```

The analysis shows that only part of the protocol can be explained by the model. In fact only actual program construction steps are modelled and other processes (e.g. analysis of the algorithm, evaluation of the partial program) are not part of the model.

8.3.5 Conclusion

Since this study used both *products* of problem-solving (in the form of answer to exam questions and solutions produced by students during practical programming work) and think aloud protocols, a comparison can be made between the analysis of products and of protocols. The main difference is that the protocols never consist of a direct path from the problem to the program.

There were always several attempted solutions, some of which were written down but others were just mentioned, evaluated and rejected. In many cases the final solution tells very little about the problem-solving process.

As illustrated by the analysis above, parts of the protocols can be explained by false implementation rules. The result of this study was that support was found for the model but that a large part of the protocols involved other processes than those predicted by the model.

8.4 Acquisition of medical knowledge

8.4.1 Example: a medical diagnosis task

In the context of the development of an advice system for an ambulance service we studied decision making by doctors. The task is to decide if an ambulance must be dispatched on the basis of an interview by telephone. This situation does not allow application of the think aloud method '*in vivo*', so we presented the interview data on a sheet of paper to experts from the medical faculty and asked them to take a decision while thinking aloud about the case.

This problem is non-standard for these experts, because they work in a hospital setting where much extra information is available (in particular data about electrocardiogram, blood pressure data and physical examination). They found this task very difficult. The number of attributes is about 40 (not all attributes apply to each case). There were only three possible decisions: decide to send an ambulance, decide that medical attention is needed but that it is not necessary that the patient is taken to hospital by ambulance, or decide that no immediate action is needed. In this version of the task all data are available to the decision maker, a cardiologist, and he is free to use them in any order. The data for one patient are listed in Appendix D. The task analysis in this case used the following information:

(a) A superficial inspection of several protocols, one of which is reproduced in Appendix D. This was the basis of the process model.
(b) A study of the medical literature. Many concepts and diagnostic rules could be obtained directly from the literature. This was a problematic and time-consuming exercise because of differences in terminology and the organization of medical knowledge by disease states and processes rather than diagnostic use. Many books, for example, discuss causes and varieties of heart diseases and the knowledge that is directly useful for diagnosis is spread out and sometimes completely missing.

(c) Existing models of diagnostic reasoning. This also inspired the process model.

8.4.2 Knowledge structures

In an earlier stage of the project, the information about the patient that is possibly relevant in the context of sudden chest pain had been collected from interviews and a study of the literature. From this information those items were selected that can reasonably be requested in a telephone interview. Also, many possible diagnoses were collected. The most important are: *heart infarction, angina pectoris, tachycardia, pulmonary embolism, non-organic chest pain* (i.e. no medical cause for the complaints). It is possible to find more specific diagnoses, but this level is specific enough to make a decision. The first requires urgent treatment. Two other, pulmonary embolism and angina pectoris, also require treatment, but the situation is (generally) less urgent. Neither the list of possible diagnoses nor the list of possibly relevant patient data is exhaustive. We found that from time to time someone would raise a possible diagnosis that had not been considered and that required additional patient information.

How can we structure the knowledge involved in this diagnostic task? We make a distinction between *patient data*, *decisions* and *diagnoses*. The relation between patient data and diagnoses is rather complex. Almost all data are associated with more than one diagnosis. In fact, many complaints and symptoms can have completely different causes. Medical textbooks and interviews with experts show that many concepts are used in the domain. Here we describe the most important types with some examples. This is an informal version of task analysis.

Patient data: The attributes to be used here were the result of an earlier stage in the analysis. See Appendix D for a list of these data. Examples are: the patient has pain in the chest, the patient has difficulties in breathing (dyspnoea), and the patient is female.

Decisions: The decisions are sending an ambulance or not. In the latter case the caller is either advised to consult one's doctor immediately or told his or her complaints require no urgent treatment, but that it is probably good to see the family doctor.

Diagnoses: In many cases, the decision is based on a preliminary diagnosis and an estimate of the severity. Diagnoses in this task are: heart infarction, angina pectoris, pulmonary embolism, non-organic chest pain and several other less frequent categories. Diagnoses can be organized in classes. For example,

important classes are *ischaemic diseases*, *cardiac diseases* and *afflicted thorax*.
Diagnostic classes: The diagnoses are often organized in hierarchies. Here we give part of a possible structure:

```
urgent
  urgent-cardiac
    ischaemic
      heart infarction*

medical attendance required
  pulmonary embolism*
  anginous
    angina pectoris*

not urgent
  not-urgent-cardiac
    tachycardia*
  thorax
    muscles
    bones
  non-organic chest pain*
```

Here the concepts marked with * are diagnoses and the other are diagnostic classes. This structure is currently incomplete. For example, the thorax diagnoses are not elaborated.

Interpretation of attributes: From attributes, interpretations can be derived. For example, the attributes 'does the dyspnoea get worse with moving' and 'does the dyspnoea get worse with a deep sigh' are very similar in meaning. If both are positive they indicate a pulmonary cause and if both are negative they exclude it. If one is positive and one is negative, it is uncertain. These two attributes can therefore be combined into a single new internal attribute, which reduces the number of attributes needed for further reasoning. In this case, domain knowledge is needed to find the interpretations. This domain knowledge was obtained in the task analysis stage. It is unlikely to be complete, because the expert may well make interpretations that are not part of textbook knowledge. We cannot give an exhaustive list of the interpretations that were found in task analysis, but we can give a few examples (in informal language):

```
IF dyspnoeic pain AND
   NOT pleural irritation AND
   NOT hyperventilation AND
   NOT high CO2 level
THEN ischaemic_pain

IF stiff fingers OR
   pain: pins and needles OR
   pain: prickling OR
   pain: burning
THEN high CO2 level
```

In general we shall refer to terms such as 'serious', 'cardiac', 'pleural irritation' as *concepts*. Concepts are used to state *conclusions* about a patient: if it is established that a patient has a 'cardiac' diagnosis, then this is a *conclusion* about the patient.

We have described the relations between concepts in symbolic, non-numerical terms. It is possible that people know weights or statistical data about these relations. Some of these data can be found in the literature, but certainly not all. We do not know (during task analysis) which of these data the expert knows.

8.4.3 The problem-solving process

Now that we have described the knowledge that can be used for this task, we turn to the problem-solving process. On the basis of the types of knowledge, we distinguish the following types of reasoning steps:

1. Inference steps: The inferences can be further classified by antecedent and conclusion (attributes, interpretations, diagnostic classes, diagnoses, decisions), but for our purpose this is not essential. The task analysis will have given a table saying for each of these concepts, if an attribute is a positive indication, a counterindication or neutral with respect to each concept. For example:

Taxonomic reasoning: Diagnostic classes are organized in a taxonomy. Inferences about concepts that are in a hierarchy have implications for other items in the hierarchy. For example, the diagnostic class 'not serious' covers several more specific diagnostic classes and specific diagnoses. Taxonomic reasoning means making inferences using properties of the taxonomy.

2. Recognize inconsistency: An inconsistency occurs when there is both positive and negative evidence for a conclusion.
3. Resolve inconsistency: This can be done in several ways:

Use extra knowledge to discard premise: Although an attribute or intermediate conclusion may in general have predictive value for another conclusion, this may not be so in a particular situation. In a particular context a conclusion may be explained by some other interpretation. Recognizing either the new conclusion or the old one that is inconsistent with it involves finding a possible interpretation and testing that. This involves extra knowledge and may cause requests for extra information or re-examination of old information.
Request extra information (to resolve inconsistency): This request can be observed as looking back over the sheet with data, retrieving information from memory or invoking extra concepts.
Take decision: This means that the inconsistent evidence is somehow used to come to a decision without really resolving the inconsistency.
Postpone: Wait until new information makes it possible to resolve the problem.

To resolve inconsistencies makes it necessary to retrieve the arguments that are involved in the contradiction. This may be difficult to do without appropriate intermediate structures. It is also a potential cause of errors, because arguments may fail to be retrieved. The actions to resolve inconsistencies may use knowledge that has not been used before.

The overall process structure is determined by the way in which the attributes are handled. Because there are many data about the patient and because these must be read by the expert there will be a stepwise process in which a new piece of information is used to update the current knowledge. A possible process structure is given in Figure 8.1.

A procedural model can be used to generate a *predicted protocol*. This is a protocol that is obtained by applying the model to a problem. If the model is a full computational model it can be run on an example and generate a solution trace that corresponds to a protocol. Models that are less formal or that do not contain full details of the knowledge involved can also be used to generate predicted protocols. An example of a predicted protocol for this task is given in Section 8.4.5.

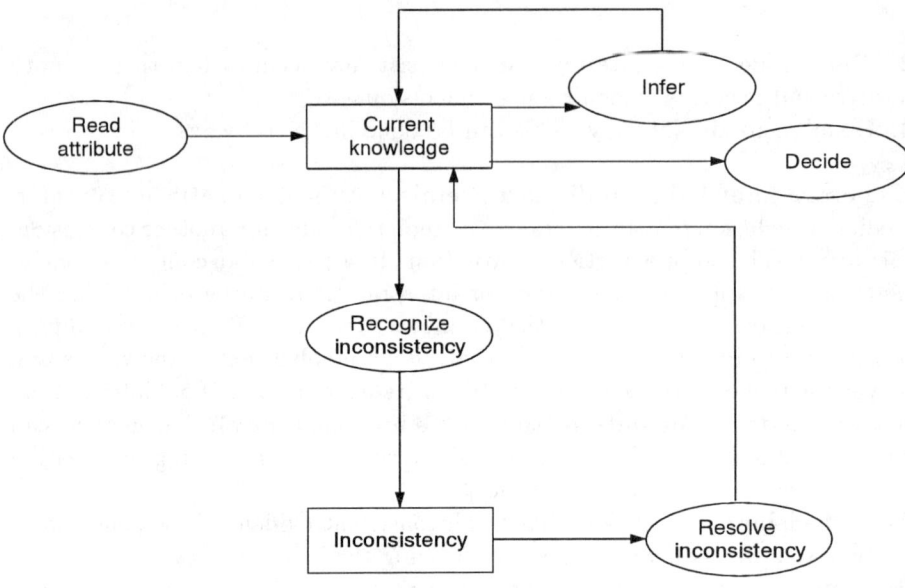

FIGURE 8.1: Model of diagnostic problem-solving

8.4.4 Alternative models

We have not discussed all possibilities for the problem solving process. For example, another process structure would be to work 'backward' from the diagnostic classes. One could exclude or verify diagnostic classes or specific diagnoses by selectively examining the data. Since our expert is not used to these forms and does not know precisely the attributes that are used, this strategy is less likely here. A full task analysis would include these. The scope of alternatives is partially determined by the knowledge that we may expect from our expert and by the intended scope of the system: should it be able to give explanations? Which range of cases should it be able to diagnose? Although the context of this example is knowledge acquisition and not a psychological study, psychological knowledge is relevant here because psychological factors determine the way in which a human expert will perform the task. This knowledge will allow a knowledge engineer to abstract from these factors and will help to decide which part of the model is worth including in the computer system. Factors that were important in architectural design also are important in medical diagnosis, in particular the capacity of working memory and the knowledge that the expert has acquired with respect to this particular task.

8.4.5 Predicted and actual protocol

In this section we address two issues: (1) How the model can be used to explain problem-solving behaviour in the form of a predicted protocol and (2) how it acts as a source of information about the domain. To illustrate the explanatory power of the model, we first show a predicted protocol and then the real protocol, discussing the discrepancies and the way in which the protocol can provide new information. The first part of the case description of the patient:

(1) Sex: female
(2) Age: 30-40 years
(3) Complaints: palpitations
dyspnoea
tired
(4) How long has the patient had dyspnoea? over 4 hours
(5) Has the patient had this dyspnoea ever before? yes

For the complete case description we refer to Appendix D. Next we show the first part of the protocol predicted by the model. This predicted protocol takes the first three lines of the case description as input. In the left column a short indication is given of the patient data. The middle column contains the content of the working memory. In the right column we list the explanations and knowledge that are used in the reasoning step.

Predicted protocol:

Patient data	Working memory	Knowledge used
1. Sex: female	sex: female	
2. Age: 30-40	sex: female age: 30-40 not urgent	sex: female and age: 30-40 $\Rightarrow$ not urgent
3. Complaints: palpitations	sex: female age: 30-40	sex: female and age: 30-40 and palpitations $\Rightarrow$

	not urgent palpitations non-organic	possibly non-organic chest pain non-organic chest pain ⇒ not urgent
	sex: female age: 30-40 not urgent palpitations non-organic tachycardia	sex: female and age: 30-40 and palpitations ⇒ possibly tachycardia tachycardia ⇒ not urgent
dyspnoea	sex: female age: 30-40 not urgent palpitations non-organic tachycardia dyspnoea	This fills up working memory. Subject will drop one item or replace several items by a new concept. Items that will be dropped can be those that were used least frequently and long ago (sex: female or age 30-40) or those that are now redundant. Taking the first we would get:
	age: 30-40 not urgent palpitations non-organic tachycardia dyspnoea	
tired	not urgent palpitations non-organic tachycardia dyspnoea tired	palpitations and dyspnoea and tired ⇒ possibly non-organic chest pain palpitations and dyspnoea and tired ⇒ possibly tachycardia

The subject in this case is a cardiologist. He is an expert on heart diseases but is not used to this type of patient data. In practice he always has at least some results of physical examination and he can see the patient and talk to him or her directly. Next we show a fragment of the actual protocol:

```
1:  This is a woman between 30 and 40 years old
2:  so I think that it's probably not too serious.
3:  ... uhh Patient has palpitations,
4:  is dyspnoeic and tired,
5:  and that are symptoms from what I think,
6:  they don't really belong to uhh cardiac complaints.
7:  ... This could be uhh a more non-organic chest pain kind of
    patient.
8:  Palpitations do occur with women of that age as tachycardia
9:  but then you should see the cardiogram.
```

As you can see, the predicted protocol and the actual protocol up to line 8 correspond rather well. In line 9 the expert says that he could use some more information, namely a cardiogram, but this is not available. This information would be needed in order to make a conclusive diagnosis. However, this is not called for by the task.

The next bit of information read by the cardiologist is that the patient has dyspnoea for over four hours, and that she had it before. The protocol continues as follows:

```
10: This dyspnoea is has been going on for more than four hours
11: so it is probably not very urgent ... but ...
12: everything is possible.
13: She has had this dyspnoea before,
14: but still, this doesn't tell me very much because
15: this might have happened one day ago, but also five
    years ago,
16: so I don't know what to do with this information,
17: I would like to ask when she has had this dyspnoea before.
```

Here we see a situation where the cardiologist needs additional information to be able to use the patient data on dyspnoea for diagnosing the cause of the patient's complaints. So far, the cardiologist inferred that the complaints were unlikely to be caused by a serious heart problem (lines 6-8). The reason that more data about the dyspnoea are given is that dyspnoea might be an indication for a lung problem (pulmonary embolism), and in this case medical treatment is required. So there might be an inconsistency at this stage between the content of the working memory *not urgent* and the new hypothesis that medical treatment is needed because of pulmonary embolism. The cardiologist tries to resolve this conflict by asking for additional information.

In task analysis a clear distinction is made between dyspnoea and pain in the chest. However, somewhat further on in the protocol the expert says:

```
24:  She's having pain and this pain has been going on
25:  for more than four hours as well,
26:  and this makes me wonder if the pain and the dyspnoea are
     somehow related,
27:  because, if they both last for longer than four hours
28:  they might be the same thing,
29:  but then the patient is unable to distinguish
30:  between the concept of pain and the concept of dyspnoea.
```

In this fragment, the expert assumes a communication problem: the subject describes a single dyspnoea and pain instead of two different symptoms. This is not what we expected in the task analysis. This kind of information can only be derived by studying actual protocols of problem-solving experts.

8.4.6 Results

This example illustrates how both domain specific knowledge can be extracted from protocols and how additional problem solving processes can be discovered from a protocol. Knowledge in the form of production rules can be extracted from the protocol basically by taking the content of working memory and the action at a particular step and turning this into a rule. In a later stage the rules must be analysed. In some cases this gives rules that were already known from the task analysis, but in other cases new events take place. In the protocol above, a new process was discovered that was not found in the task analysis. The expert hypothesizes that the patient refers to a single feeling as both *pain* and *dyspnoea*. This is a matter of language rather than a medical issue, but it is actually quite important and the protocol suggests how such a reference problem may be detected and resolved.

Resolving terminological problems has its own type of inference, but is similar to resolving inconsistencies. Because segments from an episode about terminology are coded as a step in resolving inconsistencies, some sequences in the protocol do not fit the model.

8.4.7 Conclusion

This analysis illustrates a possible use of think aloud protocols in knowledge acquisition. This analysis was one of the elements on which an advice system for the ambulance service was based. The final system has a structure similar to that used in the analysis of the protocol, although finally a different conceptual structure was used. The system is described by Post et al. (1993).

Appendix A

Exercises

A.1 Exercise 1: collecting verbal data

The purpose of this exercise is to practice procedures for collecting verbal data, in particular think aloud protocols and retrospective protocols, to obtain experience with transcribing a protocol and to find out what it means to be a subject in a think aloud experiment.

For this exercise you can use any problem-solving task that is compatible with thinking aloud. In Appendix B you find instructions for two tasks: *waterjugs* and *improving technical devices*. In addition to the materials for the task, you need a cassette recorder. You also need the help of an assistant, who can think aloud and who can assist you when you think aloud yourself.

Do the following:

1. Extend the instruction for the problem-solving task with an instruction for the think aloud procedure. Consider the possibility of a warming up for the think aloud procedure. Explain the instruction to your assistant.
2. Take two think aloud protocols of two problems within the same task domain (either waterjugs or improving devices). You are the subject and your assistant should lead the session.
3. Take two retrospective protocols of two problems in the same task domain. Again, you are the subject.
4. Now your assistant solves two waterjug problems while thinking aloud.
5. Finally your assistant solves two improving devices problems while thinking aloud.

6. Transcribe about four pages of the recorded think aloud protocols.

From this experience answer the following questions:

(a) Did the verbalizations change, for example as a result of practice ?
(b) Are there differences between the think aloud protocols and the retrospective protocols? If so, are these consistent with those discussed in Chapter 2?
(c) Would it be possible to obtain these data with interviews?
(d) Does thinking aloud have an effect on the problem-solving process?
(e) Which information is lost by transcription from the tape?
(f) As far as you can tell, do the protocols reflect the cognitive process?

A.2 Exercise 2: applicability of the think aloud method

In order to design an experiment to obtain data about a cognitive process you need to define, beside the cognitive process, the following elements: a set of problems, a verbalization procedure and subjects. The cognitive process should occur when the task is performed by these subjects and the method should provide valid and complete data about the process. Examples of cognitive processes are overcoming impasses (in problem-solving), making assumptions about unknown information or integrating large amounts of information. These processes can occur in the context of tasks such as computer programming, bird watching, legal decision making, predicting money exchange rates, selecting personnel and planning a meal. For each process, in the context of particular task, find a suitable set of problems, a suitable type of subjects and an appropriate technique for collecting data about the process.

A.3 Exercise 3: task analysis and model construction

A.3.1 Introduction

The purpose of this exercise is to practise task analysis and construction of psychological models. This example is taken from a study by Van Daalen-Kapteijns & Elshout-Mohr (1981). They studied a task in which verbal skills may be involved, namely *learning the meaning of new words* from texts in which these new words are used in context. Their main research questions were: (1) are verbally gifted persons more able to infer word meanings than others and (2) if so, in what respect does their approach to the task differ from those less verbally able? The extent to which people are 'verbally gifted' was measured by a specific intelligence test.

Their research showed that the answer to the first question is yes. Verbally able persons are indeed more proficient in inferring word meanings from texts than others. To analyse in what way they differ from others, Van Daalen-Kapteijns and Elshout-Mohr did a follow-up investigation in which protocol analysis was used.

On the basis of a first set of protocols the researchers hypothesized that the difference in performance is mainly determined by a different problem-solving method when performing the task. The main difference is that persons of low verbal skills tend to *substitute* the unknown word by a familiar word or expression, whereas the verbally able persons try to infer the main *characteristics* of the meaning of the new word and adapt these to all new information they get. As a result of this less able persons forget information that was given in earlier sentences or that was inferred before. Therefore they need to go back to earlier sentences more often. Another effect is that they may give a solution to the problem that is not consistent with all sentences. This results in poor solutions or long solution times.

A.3.2 Example problem

Here follows the instruction for the task and part of a think aloud protocol. Subjects have a sheet of paper on which they can take notes. The subjects' notes are at the bottom of the episode during which they were made. For example the note '`Kolper can be part of a room`' was made after reading sentence 1 and before reading sentence 2.

Instruction for the subjects

This study investigates the way people handle texts in which words unknown to them are used. Before you, you have five little cards. At the back of each card a sentence is written, using the same unknown word. Your task is to figure out what each sentence means and then to infer valid information about the meaning of the new word. We ask you to think aloud while doing the task. Note any information you find out about the unknown word down on the pad before you.

Two further remarks:

1. The new words used in this experiments have complex meanings that can

only be captured in one or more sentences. None of the words can be substituted by a single existing word.
2. It may happen that a new word reminds you of another word which sounds the same. Try not to go by such likeness, because sound kinship does not necessarily imply kinship of meaning.

Problem

Sentence 1: A room with one or two kolpers on a court is not very attractive.

Sentence 2: During a heatwave many people long for kolpers so the sale of marquees reaches a record.

Sentence 3: The ad stresses the fact that the room is facing south, but just on the south side the room has kolpers.

Sentence 4: Although this room certainly does not have kolpers, it is so deep that you need to turn the light on, during the day as well, on clouded days.

Sentence 5: Those large trees along the canals are indisputably very beautiful but as a consequence many canal-houses have to put up with kolpers all summer.

A.3.3 Suggestions for task analysis and psychological model

The basic structure of the task can be characterized as follows:

Goal: a definition that has approximately the following structure:
A `<target word>` is a `<concept/noun>` that is a `<description>` of particular properties distinguishing `<target word>` from `<concept>`.
For example, a possible solution for the problem above is ' A `kolper is a window that cannot be reached by the sunlight`'.
Givens:
(a) Directly given properties. These are properties of the target concept that are given directly in the text.
(b) Inferred properties. These are not given directly in the text but can be inferred. For example, the phrase *during a heat wave people long for kolpers* suggests the property that *kolpers* reduce heat, although this is not stated di-

directly but is inferred from the given properties.

The process of finding word meanings may use the following pieces of information:
• Current set of properties consisting of both inferred and directly given properties.
• Current concept.

Also, the process may consist of:
• Inferring new properties.
• Integrating new properties into the current set.
• Constructing a tentative definition.

Integrating new properties involves handling possible inconsistencies. For example, suppose that the current set of properties of *kolper* is:
`part of room, furniture, size at least size of chair, reduces heat (during heatwave)`
and a new property is `a kind of window`. This is inconsistent with the property `furniture`. This inconsistency must be resolved by revising either `furniture` or `a kind of window`.

The psychological hypothesis is that poor performance on this task is caused by a weak method for updating the current property set. There are two important properties of possible strategies:

Revision versus replacing: Start with an initial property set. If this is inconsistent with a new property then drop the initial property set and construct a new one from the current text. The drawback is of course that this does not maintain consistency with the previous texts. The advantage is that it avoids the revision process which can be difficult, because it requires retrieving the justification for the inconsistent properties and revising this, which may affect other properties.

Size of the property set: A text may contain several properties and it may be possible to infer quite a few more from the text and the other current properties. Revision or replacing can involve few properties (e.g. two: a concept with one discriminative property) or more. More properties require more reasoning during the updating process.

The most elaborate strategy consists of full *revision with a maximal property set*. The strategy involving the least resources is *replacing with a minimal property set*. If resources allow application of the first strategy the result is likely to be better, because full use is made of all available information. The hypothesis is that better performers will follow the better strategy and poor performers the simpler and poorer strategy.

A.3.4 Exercise

In appendix C two segmented think aloud protocols are reproduced. Do the following:

1. Make a **task analysis**. Limit the scope of the analysis to what is relevant for the research issues and to what can be expected to appear in protocols. First try to make the task analysis without looking at the protocols. If that fails, use one of the protocols as a pilot protocol.
2. Apply the psychological hypothesis to the task analysis to obtain a **psychological model**. The model should be detailed enough to allow the construction of a coding scheme later on. Make a model for each type of problem-solving behaviour. The models should clearly reflect the hypothesized differences between novices and experts and people with high and low verbal skills.
3. Construct a coding scheme.
4. Code the given protocols and have someone else do the same with the same coding scheme.
5. Determine the inter-coder reliability of the two codings.
6. Use the coded protocols to answer the question that motivated the analysis.
7. Try to collect new protocols from subjects that are similar to those used in these experiments, to collect your own protocols and analyse these with the coding scheme.
8. Discuss the implications of the results of the analysis for the research question.
9. Discuss the difficulties in applying the think aloud method and consider alternative methods.

A.4   Exercise 4: knowledge acquisition

Appendix D gives the full protocol of a medical diagnosis problem, part of which was discussed in Chapter 8. Continue the analysis given in Chapter 8 with the rest of the protocol. Construct a psychological model for this task, as far as possible. Since you are probably not an expert yourself this model will be very incomplete with respect to the actual knowledge that is used. Use the protocol to complete your model and to check if it is complete. Revise the model on the basis of the protocol.

A.5   Exercise 5: physics problem solving

In Chapter 8 we discussed a model of advanced problem solving in physics. In Appendix F you find a think aloud protocol of a novice subject (translated from Dutch into English). Code the protocol in terms of the model and compare the protocol with the model. Use the analysis to check Jansweijer's hypothesis about the differences between advanced and novice problem solvers.

Appendix B

Instructions for two problem-solving tasks

B.1   Task 1: waterjug problems

For this task you only need paper and pencil. There are several variations of the basic task. Here we give the instruction:
You have two waterjugs. One jug can hold 5 litres and the other 3 litres. The jugs have no marks and one cannot see how much water they contain. They can be filled from a water tap and emptied in a sink. One can also pour water from one jug in another. Is that clear ?
We ask you to note the contents of the waterjug on this sheet. Please make two columns, one for each jug. Initially, both jugs are empty, so we have 0 - 0. Is that clear? Your task is to make 4 litres of water.

It is easy to make variations by changing the target amount, the volume of the jugs and also the number of jugs.

B.2   Task 2: improving technical devices

The instruction for the task 'improving technical devices' reads as follows:
This task consists of inventing improvements for technical devices. I shall give you the name of a technical device and your task is to invent five improvements of this device.

Some possible devices are: *washing machine, telephone* and *elevator*.

Appendix C

Protocols of 'learning word meanings'

C.1 Protocol 1

```
 1:  [reads sentence 1]
 2:  oh ... when you find yourself
 3:  ... in a room with 1 or 2 kolpers on a court
 4:  ... well, it evidently is something depressing
 5:  something that takes away the view
 6:  ... er ...
 7:  with 1 or 2
 8:  although, not necessarily so
 9:  ... because a room on a court means having no view at all
10:  ... so, strictly speaking that does not say anything
11:  ... it has something to do with a room ...
12:  I am looking whether kolpers is linked to room or court
13:  ... a room with 1 or 2 kolpers on a court
14:  ... I think it means something like windows or so
15:  like a room with 1 or 2 windows on a court
16:  but I don't understand why they put 1 or 2 windows because
17:  that would imply that there could well be other windows
18:  that do provide a large view
19:  ... first write down what I know now
20:  ... it has something to do with a room
```

```
21:  I think one could say that its a part
22:  ... of the room [starts writing]
23:  a kolper can
24:  ... I have to say 'can be' because it can as easily be part
     of something else
25:  ... can be part of a room.
```

Note: Kolper can be part of a room

```
26   [reads sentence 2]
27:  many people long for kolpers
28:  that could mean that it is
29:  ... er is kind of shut off window
30:  or a window being in the shade
31:  that would be congruent with the last sentence with that
     depressing bit
32:  maybe it means something like a window blocked by a wall
33:  ... right in front
34:  not permitting a view ... er and is cool ...
35:  during something like a heatwave
36:  ... er ...
37:  I can't infer much new information
38:  I just note down that it has something to do with a room
39:  ... er ...
40:  now I am looking at this sentence's construction again
41:  ... who are the ones longing for kolpers
42:  ... if a kolper were a window in the shade or something
     like that
43:  they would not have to buy marquees
44:  maybe it are the shops or something that are longing for
     kolpers ...
45:  actually this sentence makes it less clear
46:  except that I now know that it has something to do with a
     window
47:  I don't know much else ...
```

Note: a kolper has something to do with a room

```
48:  [reads sentence 3]
49:  this reminds me immediately of a window without a view or
```

```
       something
50:    or a wall just in front of it
51:    er ... maybe more precise ...
52:    something that is in the shadow ...
53:    because on the south side you would expect sunlight in the
       room
54:    and if that's just the place where the kolpers are
55:    then it could mean something like a window
56:    which permits no light to come through
57:    but then I do not understand the previous sentence very well
58:    ... oh, now I suddenly do understand the previous sentence
59:    ... it is that people long for shadowed windows
60:    and therefore they buy marquees ...
61:    so I will just write that down ...
62:    a kolper seems to be a shadowed window or something ...
63:    [writes] ...
64:    I believe that that's it
65:    that one can say nothing more about it ...
66:    it may, but is not necessarily shadowed by a house in front
67:    it may but needs not be
68:    but it may as well be by marquees and so er ...
69:    see what have I got now: shadowed room ...
70:    yes that is it ...

Note: A kolper seems to be a shadowed window
```

C.2 Protocol 2

```
1:    [reads sentence 1]
      a room with two kolpers on a court is not very attractive
2:    let me go back to this
3:    what am I supposed to do
4:    it is in there
5:    I see, OK
6:    two kolpers on a court is not very attractive ...
7:    it doesn't suggest anything to me offhand except that
8:    let's see
9:    two things on a court
```

10: could possibly produce some kind of a crowding situation
11: or let's see what else could be unattractive about it
12: could be some conflict
13: maybe I don't know
14: if crowding is the thing that makes them very unattractive
15: perhaps they are very large
16: each kolper is rather large
17: and putting two together crowds the space somehow
18: or else they are belligerent
   [writes]
19: they may fight when they are together
20: so ... it doesn't specify it for me
21: so let's see
22: what am I supposed to do
23: I still don't quite understand
24: what it is that I am supposed to do
25: figure out what the sentence means
26: well the meaning of the sentence is not so difficult in this case
27: a room with two objects of some
28: two kolpers on a court
29: how about the room
30: a room with something on a court
31: it doesn't make very much sense to me
32: a room on a court ...

Note: belligerent, crowded

E: perhaps you should have a look at the next sentence

33: [reads sentence 2]
   during a heatwave many people long for kolpers, so the sale of marquees reaches a record
34: well, let's see
35: this is, this gives some some relief
36: kolpers, a kolper gives a relief from heat
37: marquee, a marquee has something to do ...
38: the sale of marquees
39: a marquee is a kind of ...
40: if there is a heatwave signs appear advertising these things

Example: learning word meanings

41: because they somehow give relief from the heat
42: alright
43: that still doesn't specify it very precisely
44: it could be any number of things I suppose
45: relief from the heat
46: it could be a cold place to go
47: an airconditioned ...
48: I don't know
49: sale of marquees
50: do I get to look at another one

E: yes, you just turn over the sheet

51: [reads sentence 3]
   the ad stresses the fact that the room is facing south but just on the south side the room has kolpers
52: usually south facing rooms would be warmer than north facing rooms
53: not necessarily, but it might be
54: but the thing is that at the south side the room has these kolpers
55: and the kolpers are things that appear to have
56: something to do with unpleasant heat

57: [reads sentence 4]
   although this room certainly does not have kolpers it is so deep that you have to turn on the light, during the day as well, on clouded days
58: this is also rather puzzling because
59: the very first one refers to the kolpers being on a court
60: two kolpers on a court
61: now, wouldn't normally ...
62: saying a room has two such and such on a court
63: that sentence suggests a room facing on a court
64: so, a space outside the room
65: so the kolpers are not in the room
66: but the sentence number 4 seems to ...
67: now OK, the room does not have kolpers
68: this room does not have kolpers
69: that means that some room might have them

70: isn't that impossible
71: but in any case the room is very deep
72: and that has something to do with this whole story
73: maybe because if you turn the light on it gets warmer
74: let's see

75: [reads sentence 5]
    those large trees on the canals are indisputably very beautiful but as a consequence many canalhouses have to put up with kolpers all summer
76: OK, let's look what I can make out of this
77: to put up with these things all summer so these are
78: so these things appear only during summer
79: I am not getting a picture of what these things could be
80: except that they are not err ...
81: let's see
82: I have the impression from what is stated there
83: these things wherever they are
84: are not found in rooms
85: are maybe seen from rooms
86: but then again I am not sure because sentence number 4 suggests
87: because it says although this room certainly does not have kolpers
88: now that conditional phrase suggests some rooms might possibly have them
89: this one certainly does not have them
90: and some rooms might have them
91: OK, but if they are something that you look out on
92: then if that were true
93: you wouldn't normally expect to find them in a room at all
94: but let me see
95: what information do I actually have
96: OK, looking out on these things is not attractive
97: what else can I put that together with
98: people long for them during heatwaves
99: so it has something to do with avoiding heat
100: so my initial thought of why they are unattractive
101: may well or may not be the case
102: OK perhaps a kolper is some kind of a space

103: in which you can cool off
104: OK that might be a consistent interpretation
105: it could perhaps be an enclosure of some kind
106: that is found on the water or on a canal
107: maybe, I don't know
108: because that would explain the advertisements during heatwaves
109: as is often the case with temporary structures it might be unattractive
110: maybe a small one is tolerable
111: so that might explain the first sentence
112: so perhaps it is some ...
113: my conclusion is that it is some kind of structure
114: that is not especially attractive
115: and that if you have more than one in the same area
116: and if you look out on such things
117: you talk about things that are not pleasant to look at

Appendix D

Analysing expert problem-solving

In Chapter 8 we gave an example from a medical domain. Below we reproduce the case description and a full protocol.

D.1 Case description

(1)	Sex:	female
(2)	Age:	30-40 years
(3)	Complaints:	palpitations
		dyspnoea
		tired
(4)	How long has the patient had dyspnoea?	over 4 hours
(5)	Has the patient had this dyspnoea ever before?	yes
(6)	Does the dyspnoea get worse with a deep sigh?	no
(7)	Does the dyspnoea get worse when moving?	no
(8)	Does the patient have pain?	yes
(9)	How long has the patient had pain?	over 4 hours
(10)	Where is the pain?	left in the chest
(11)	Does the patient feel the pain anywhere else?	no
(12)	Has the patient had this feeling ever before?	yes

(13)	What was the patient doing at that time?	quiet
(14)	Did the patient use tongue tablets for this?	no
(15)	Did the patient use those tablets this time?	no
(16)	Is the pain at the same place as before?	yes
(17)	Is the feeling the same as before?	yes
(18)	Does the pain get worse with a deep sigh?	no
(19)	Does the pain change with movement?	no
(20)	How strong is the pain?	somewhat strong
(21)	Does the patient feel sick?	no
(22)	Does the patient sweat?	no
(23)	Is the patient under treatment by a cardiologist or internist?	yes
(24)	Has the patient ever before had a heart infarction?	no
(25)	Are there members of the patients family who have had a heart infarction at an early age?	yes
(26)	Does the patient smoke more than five cigarettes a day?	no
(27)	Has the patient done this a short time ago?	no
(28)	Does the patient have high blood pressure (hypertension)?	yes
(29)	Does the patient have diabetes?	no
(30)	What does the patient think that is wrong?	the heart

D.2 Protocol

```
1:   This is a woman between 30 and 40 years old
2:   so I think that it's probably not too serious.
3:   ... uhh Patient has palpitations,
4:   is dyspnoea and tired,
5:   and that are symptoms from what I think,
6:   they don't really belong to uhh cardiac complaints.
7:   ... This could be uhh a more non-organic chest pain kind of
     patient.
8:   Palpitations do occur with women of that age as tachycardia
9:   but then you should see the cardiogram.
10:  This dyspnoea is has been going on for more than four hours
11:  so it is probably not very urgent ... but ...
12:  everything is possible.
13:  She has had this dyspnoea before,
```

```
14: but still, this doesn't tell me very much because
15: this might have happened one day ago, but also five years
    ago,
16: so I don't know what to do with this information,
17: I would like to ask when she has had this dyspnoea before.
18: ... uhh The pain doesn't get worse when she is sighing
    deeply.
19: ... That can be interpreted as evidence against pulmonary
    embolism,
20: uhh dyspnoea doesn't get worse when she's moving.
21: When the dyspnoea gets worse if the person is moving
22: that would suggest problems with the muscles or the bones
23: of the thorax, but this doesn't look like that.
24: She's having pain and this pain has been going on
25: for more than four hours as well,
26: and this makes me wonder if the pain and the dyspnoea are
    somehow related,
27: because, if they both last for longer than four hours
28: they might be the same thing,
29: buh then the patient is unable to distinguish
30: between the concept of pain and the concept of dyspnoea.
31: The pain is on the left side of the chest.
32: From this we also know that this is
33: no evidence for angina pectoris or ischaemia in any case.
34: There is no pain in other places,
35: so there is no pain in the arms or in the chest.
36: She has had this feeling before, then in rest.
37: ... uhh ... This is strange because pain and dyspnoea
    in rest
38: are usually not anginuous and ... then what matters is,
39: if we're talking about the pain
40: and the pain occurs during rest,
41: then it might be an infarction.
42: ... Now I see,
43: suddenly we're talking about this feeling.
44: This feeling refers to,
45: We are talking about both dyspnoea and pain
46: and I don't know what this feeling actually means.
47: This patient has had this feeling before,
48: ... you have to be more specific about this.
```

49: What do you mean, dyspnoea or pain.
50: Anyway, she has had it before during rest
51: and, I think that this is a bit strange
52: because, if it is anginuous, and it is during rest,
53: then it might be an infarction
54: but it is strange if the pain, or the dyspnoea
55: always occurs during rest, because,
56: if it is related to the heart, then it is usually not in rest.
57: ... And, if it was during rest now, and it was during rest then,
58: than it is an infarction maybe,
59: but then should it have been an infarction then,
60: and that is strange.
61: So complaints about a pain that only occurs during rest,
62: or dyspnoea, are not very strong evidence for a infarction.
63: Well, she wasn't using tablets for the tongue,
64: so she had, they probably were not prescribed.
65: She hasn't used the tablets now either.
66: Actually, the question is if she was having those tablets at all
67: You see, there is a difference between having them and using them
68: If you don't have the tablets you can't use them,
69: but if you do have those tablets you have a choice of using them
70: Do you see what I mean?
71: ... uhh Is the pain in the same place as before? Yes.
72: Well that is good, or anyway it gives a uhh
73: it is something that is consistent in the story,
74: and is it the same feeling as before?
75: That is also, the answer is yes,
76: that is also something that makes the story consistent.
77: It doesn't get worse when she is sighing deeply.
78: Why are they asking this, because
79: this has been asked as dyspnoea before.
80: Here, first it is asked if the dyspnoea gets worse
81: when she is sighing deeply and then it is asked
82: if the pain gets worse when she is sighing deeply.
83: Actually, this question isn't very suitable for dyspnoea

84: because having pain when you are sighing deeply
85: belongs to pulmonary pain and
86: pulmonary pain is interpreted, felt, as real pain.
87: We have said that both pain and dyspnoea
88: have to be seen as two words that indicate the same thing
89: because the pain of angina pectoris
90: is sometimes interpreted as dyspnoea,
91: but the pain of pulmonary pain is not something
92: that you would refer to as dyspnoea.
93: So, now actually the question if the dyspnoea gets worse
94: when she is sighing deeply is not very logical
95: if that question will return as pain when she is sighing deeply.
96: Anyway, this is not the case.
97: The pain doesn't get worse when she is moving.
98: This is the same question as about dyspnoea.
99: ... The the question is, what do you mean by moving?
100: We always meant moving arms and legs and chest,
101: and things like that, but in a way,
102: exertion is a way of moving too,
103: and that is something that we do not mean.
104: ... Well, the intensity of the pain is average.
105: She is not sick
106: she is not sweating,
107: that is not very useful information at the moment.
108: She is under treatment of a cardiologist or an internist.
109: That is strange because, why are women between 30 and 40
110: under treatment of a cardiologist or an internist.
111: So she has never had an infarction.
112: There are members of the family who have had a infarction at a young age.
113: ... uhh She doesn't smoke more than five cigarettes a day.
114: She hasn't done this before either.
115: ... uhh ...
116: Well, these are not risk factors
117: that really apply to young women.
118: That is something that starts to matter when they are, say 40, 50, 60 years old,
119: because these risk factors have to do their work for a longer time.

120: Still, we know that sometimes, but this is highly exceptional,
121: women of this age do get an infarction.
122: Well she does have a high blood pressure.
123: You would like to know what kind of high blood pressure,
124: how high I mean, and if she is getting treatment for it,
125: but that is not so relevant at this moment.
126: uhh This rises the question if this is the reason
127: that she is under treatment by a cardiologist or internist.
128: She doesn't have diabetes and
129: her own opinion is that it is her heart.
130: Well, if that is what she is thinking herself,
131: this means that she is very worried about it.
132: Maybe this is because she is under treatment of a cardiologist,
133: or maybe because she is a hearts neurotic.
134: uhh Do I know everything that I need to know?
135: uhh Concerning the medical history only,
136: I think that there is not very much left
137: that I would like to know, apart from uhh ...
138: maybe the pain that she,
139: I would like to know a bit more about the pain.
140: She says that she has had this before and
141: that it was at rest then,
142: and I would like to know if it happened
143: every day, every week, every month,
144: or that it happened only once before.
145: If I look at the story as a whole,
146: I think that it is not very likely that she,
147: that this is ischaemia
148: and I would like to ask again
149: if the pain really doesn't occur during exertion.
150: Apparently she says spontaneously
151: that the pain occurs during rest,
152: but I would like to ask
153: if the pain really doesn't occur during exertion,
154: and if she is able to exert.
155: Because, if someone is able to exert
156: and the pain only occurs during rest,
157: then that is evidence against ischaemia.

158: So, for the moment, I would like to conclude that
159: this is probably not cardiac.
160: uhh It is not impossible that she is having
161: something like a pulmonary embolism
162: but I wouldn't put my money on it.
163: I wouldn't send an ambulance.

Appendix E

Coding scheme architectural design

In this section the complete coding scheme constructed by Hamel (1990) is given. To guide the reading of the coding scheme we present again the psychological model of architectural design in Figure E.1.

Task schema level
Orientation: general comment from which appears:
O1: realization that a design task is concerned, for example: 'what am I to design?'
O2: realization of the kind of task: 'it is a new development'; 'a sort of youth centre I see'
O3: that the outside area is to be designed as well: 'so, also playgrounds'
O4: estimation of the usefulness of the data supplied
O5: estimation of the extra information needed

Execution A: general comment concerning:
X1: task-irrelevant incidents during design: 'let me answer the phone'; 'I'll order coffee'
X2: degree of difficulty, measure of effort, duration of activities: 'I'll see how far I can get in this amount of time'
X3: strategy, procedure and approach during the analysis of the task: 'let me begin by'; 'I happen just to have built such a clubhouse, what you need to have there is'
X4: materials (maps, photographs) and equipment (paper, felt-tips)

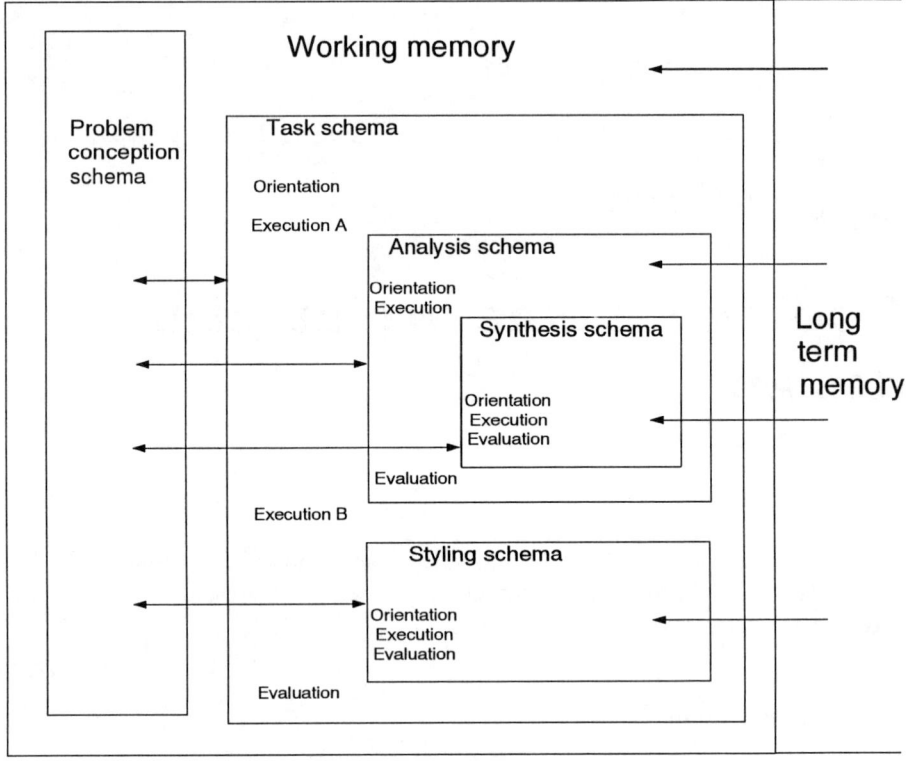

FIGURE E.1: The psychological model of architectural design

Analysis schema level
Orientation: comment showing the use of:
AO1a: task text
AO1b: task maps and drawings
AO1c: task photographs
AO1d: information supplied orally by the investigator
AO2: own knowledge
AO3: information gathered, literature
AO4: communication with the client
AO5: communication with an expert
AO6: making an assumption, estimation

Subjects the orientation is concerned with, to be permuted with AO1 through AO6:

not one specific subject:
0:      just reads

situational data:
1:      characteristics of the situation: position, urban development characteristics, zoning plan, construction characteristics, demographic data, services
2:      measurements of the situation
3:      traffic
4:      walking routes and openings in the situation
5:      position of the situation in relation to the sun
6:      concerning users: age, behaviour

task data:
7:      available budget
8:      number of users
9:      management and exploitation

task requirements:
10:    functions
11:    criteria for functions, characteristics of functions
12:    measurements for functions
13:    concerning use
14:    concerning appearance
15:    concerning technique

data, general requirements:
16:    norms, suggestions, regulations
17:    concerning use
18:    concerning technique

Execution: general comment concerning:
AX1:   strategy, procedure and approach during the synthesize of the design: 'I'll now look at the consequences of this position for the playing facilities for the little ones and for safety'
AX2:   the task as submitted: 'this task leaves rather a lot of freedom'

Synthesis schema level

Orientation:
SO1: reading through, checking, or recapitulating data, conclusions or results of actions (for example: surface areas, characteristics of functions)
SO2: estimation concerning combination of aspects of the design: 'this area seems very large for a building like this'; 'I think we'll be able to combine a few functions in one room'

Execution: comment showing one is working on:
SX1: organization diagram building, followed by SE1 or SE2
SX2: organization diagram outside area, followed by SE1 or SE2
SX3: area diagram building, followed by SE1 or SE2
SX4: area diagram outside area, followed by SE1 or SE2
SX5: construction diagram, followed by SE1 or SE2
SX6: situation, urban-developmental layout, followed by SE1 or SE2
SX7: cross-section building, followed by SE1 or SE2
SX8: cross-section outside area, followed by SE1 or SE2
SX9: isometric perspective

Evaluation:
SE1: comparison of expectations, inspection, or checking of organization diagram, area diagram, etc.: 'I'll have land to spare'; 'it's too small for the number of users, but too big for the budget available'
SE2: redesigning of organization diagram, area diagram, situation or cross-section, without check of earlier product
SE3: organization diagram, area diagram, situation, or cross-section, not followed by SE1 or SE2

Analysis schema level

Evaluation:
AE1: comparison of expectations, inspection, or checking of data or requirements
AE2: renewed deduction of data or requirements, search, etc., without check of earlier product
AE3: data or requirements, not followed by AE1 or AE2
AE4: making changes in the task

Task schema level

Execution B: general comment concerning:
- X1: task-irrelevant incidents during design: 'let me answer the phone'; 'I'll order coffee'
- X2: degree of difficulty, measure of effort, duration of activities: 'I'll see how far I can get in this space of time'
- X4: materials (maps, photographs) and equipment (paper, felt-tips)
- X5: strategy, procedure and approach in the styling of the design: 'I'll now see how to fit this nicely into this corner'

Styling schema level

Orientation:
- YO1: study of one's own sketches; read through, check, or recapitulate data, conclusions, or results of actions
- YO2: estimation concerning the appearance of the building and the situation

Execution: comment showing one is working on:
- YX1: situation, followed by YE1 or YE2
- YX2: floor plan, followed by YE1 or YE2
- YX3: cross-section, followed by YE1 or YE2
- YX4: appearance, followed by YE1 or YE2
- YX5: perspective, isometric perspective, followed by YE1 or YE2
- YX6: construction, followed by YE1 or YE2
- YX7: materials, followed by YE1 or YE2
- YX8: texture, followed by YE1 or YE2
- YX9: colours, followed by YE1 or YE2

Evaluation:
- YE1: comparison of expectations, inspection, or checking of the appearance of the situation, floor plan, etc.: 'I don't like this'
- YE2: renewed sketching, without check of earlier sketch
- YE3: situation, floor plan, cross-section, appearance, etc., not followed by YE1 or YE2

Task schema level

Evaluation: general comment concerning:
E1:   the performance of the task: quick, easy, difficult
E2:   the experimental session as a whole
E3:   explicit reflection on method, comment on the process, interpretations, generalizations and analysis of one's own thinking
E4:   remarks on expectations concerning the usefulness of data supplied and extra information obtained

Appendix F

Protocol of novice problem-solving in physics

This is the text of a complete segmented protocol of a novice problem solver. The first part of the protocol contains the literal text of the problem.

```
1:   Ideal gas is in a container
2:   that is closed by a piston
3:   the volume of the gas is 2 litres
4:   and the pressure 120 ... kilopascal
5:   by slowly moving the piston outward
6:   the volume is increased to 3 litres
7:   the temperature of the gas
8:   is kept constant
9:   what is the pressure of the gas
10:  after moving the piston
11:  well this will be less of course
12:  I mm I mm have to calculate that
```

Experimenter: yes and keep thinking aloud

```
13:  well ehhh
14:  let's see
15:  the temperature will be ehhh cons
16:  no
17:  let's first go from 2 litres
18:  to 3 litres
```

```
19:  there is a formula for that
20:  is probably in pressure
21:  calculated in pressure
22:  120 kilopascal
23:  Let's see ehh
24:  there is a formula
25:  that says P is F divided by O
26:  but that is not asked
27:  that is simply given
28:  perhaps another
29:  yes ... ehhhh ...
30:  here ...
31:  this is it ... probably
32:  I have to find a relation
33:  between pressure and volume
34:  where is it ...
35:  the problem is that this pressure
36:  is related only to surface
37:  I think that I must be here ...
38:  probably a ehh first
39:  look at the ideal gasses
40:  P is 120
41:  that is the first ... law
42:  or the first rule that ...
43:  V is RT
44:  that P is given
45:  is 120 kilopascal
46:  yes the V that is the first 2 litres
47:  times 2
48:  V is always given in litres
49:  ehh or in cubic meters? ...
50:  ehhhh ... well ...
51:  I leave that to the 2
52:  is R and that R
53:  or is it not too heav
54:  an ideal gas ... the ideal gas
55:  was 3 2 R
56:  is 3 divided by 2 ... oh
57:  then it is Cp or Cv
58:  constant pressure or constant ehh volume
```

59: it is no constant volume
60: so I use constant pressure
61: that R is ehh
62: take the universal gas constant
63: so times 8.13 ...
64: oh ... 31
65: 4
66: Joule times kelvin ... times T
67: that is the temperature
68: and that remained constant
69: so that will drop out
70: if I make another equation
71: so here we get again ehhh ...
72: this pressure must change
73: ... 2 ... is now ...
74: this must be the same
75: etcetera
76: yes 240 is
77: and then you can compute this T ...
78: shall I do that? ehh
79: 240 divided by 8.314 ... eh
80: 40 divided by ... 8 ... 14
81: divided by 5 ... times 2 ... 11.55 ...
82: so here should be 11.55 ...
83: this becomes 3
84: because that is the change
85: now, then I compute this ... ehh 5
86: divided by 2 ... divided by 3 ...
87: times 8.314 times 11.55 is ...
88: that will indeed be less
89: 80 0 2
90: now I am not certain if I ehh
91: should write litres or cubic metres
92: a litre is ... how many litres go into a cubic metre?
93: 1000 because a litre is a cubic decimetre
94: or not, no ... well it does not matter
95: it will all drop out against each other
96: this is the answer

Experimenter: 80, so 80 what?

97: let's see, P
98: and P is kilopascal
99: should be kilopascal

Bibliography

ANDERSON, J. R. (1989). A theory of the origins of human knowledge. *Artifical Intelligence*, 40:313–351.
ANDERSON, J. R. (1990). *Cognitive psychology and its implications*. W.H. Freeman, New York.
ANZAI, Y. & SIMON, H. A. (1979). A theory of learning by doing. *Psychological Review*, 86:124–140.
BARNARD, Y. F. & ERKENS, G. (1989). Simulation and analysis of problem solving and dialogue processing within co-operative learning. In Mandl, H., de Corte, E., Bennett, N., & Friedrich, H., editors, *Learning and Instruction: European research in an international context*, volume 2.1, pages 181–196. Pergamon Press, Oxford.
BREUKER, J. A. & WIELINGA, B. J. (1987). Use of models in the interpretation of verbal data. In Kidd, A. L., editor, *Knowledge Acquisition for Expert Systems, a practical handbook*, pages 17–44. Plenum Press, New York.
BROWNSTONE, L., FARRELL, R., KANT, E., & MARTIN, N. (1985). *Programming expert systems in OPS5: an introduction to rule-based programming*. Addison-Wesley, Reading, Massachusetts.
CHI, M. T. H., BASSOK, M., LEWIS, M., REIMANN, P., & GLASER, R. (1989). Self-explanations: how students study and use examples in learning to solve problems. *Cognitive Science*, 13:145–182.
CLANCEY, W. J. (1988). Acquiring, representing and evaluating a competence model of diagnosis. In Chi, M. T. H., Glaser, R., & Farr, M. J., editors, *The Nature of Expertise*, pages 343–418. Lawrence Erlbaum Associates, Hillsdale, New Jersey.
DE GROOT, A. D. (1946). *Het denken van den schaker (Thought in chess)*. PhD thesis, University of Amsterdam, Amsterdam (in Dutch).
DE GROOT, A. D. (1965). *Thought and choice in chess*. Mouton, The Hague.
DIAPER, D., editor (1989). *Knowledge Elicitation: principles, techniques and applications*. Ellis Horwood, Chichester.

DUNCKER, K. (1945). *On problem solving*. The American Psychological Association, Washington. (orig. 1935).

ERICSSON, K. A. & SIMON, H. A. (1993). *Protocol Analysis: Verbal Reports as Data (revised edition)*. MIT Press, Cambridge, Mass.

EVERITT, B. S. (1977). *The analysis of contingency tables*. Chapman and Hall, London.

FERGUSON-HESSLER, M. G. M. & DE JONG, T. (1990). Studying physics texts: differences in study processes between good and poor performers. *Cognition and Instruction*, 7:41–54.

GRUBER, T. G. (1989). Automated knowledge acquisition for strategic knowledge. *Machine Learning*, 4(3/4):293–336.

HAMEL, R. (1990). *Over het denken van de architect (On the thought processes of architects)*. AHA books, Amsterdam (in Dutch).

JACKSON, P. (1990). *Introduction to Expert Systems*. Addison-Wesley, Reading, Massachusetts.

JANSWEIJER, W. N. H. (1988). *PDP: Een benadering vanuit de kunstmatige intelligentie van probleemoplossen en leren in een semantisch rijk domein (PDP: An artificial intelligence approach to problem solving and learning by doing in a semantically rich domain)*. PhD thesis, University of Amsterdam, Amsterdam (in Dutch).

JANSWEIJER, W. N. H., ELSHOUT, J. J., & WIELINGA, B. J. (1987). The expertise of novice problem solvers. In du Boulay, B., Hogg, D., & Steels, L., editors, *Advances in Artifical Intelligence II*, pages 121–130. Elsevier Science Publishers, Amsterdam.

KINTSCH, W. & GREENO, J. G. (1985). Understanding and solving arithmetic word problems. *Psychological Review*, 92:109–129.

KUIPERS, B. & KASSIRER, J. P. (1984). Causal reasoning in medicine: Analysis of a protocol. *Cognitive Science*, 8:363–385.

KUIPERS, B., MOSKOWITZ, A. J., & KASSIRER, J. P. (1988). Critical decisions under uncertainty: Representation and structure. *Cognitive Science*, 12:177–210.

LAIRD, J. E., NEWELL, A., & ROSENBLOOM, P. S. (1987). SOAR: an architecture for general intelligence. *Artificial Intelligence*, 33:1–64.

LUCAS, P. & VAN DER GAAG, L. (1991). *Principles of expert systems*. Addison-Wesley, Reading, Massachusetts.

MAIER, N. R. F. (1931). Reasoning in humans II. The solution to a problem and its appearance in consciousness. *Journal of Comparative Psychology*, 12:181–194.

MARCUS, S., editor (1988). *Automatic knowledge acquisition for expert systems*. Kluwer, Boston.

MEYER, M. A. & BOOKER, J. M. (1991). *Eliciting and Analyzing Expert Judgement: A Practical Guide.* Academic Press, London.

MITRI, M. (1991). A task-specific problem solving architecture for candidate evaluation. *AI Magazine,* 12(3):95–109.

MORGOEV, V. K. (1989). ARIADNA: a knowledge elicitation support system. *AI Comunications,* 2(3/4):131–141.

MUSEN, M. A. (1989a). *Automated Generation of Model-Based Knowledge-Acquisition Tools.* Pitman, London.

MUSEN, M. A. (1989b). Automated support for building and extending expert models. *Machine Learning,* 4:347–376.

NEWELL, A. (1990). *Unified theories of cognition.* Harvard University Press, Cambridge, Massachusetts.

NEWELL, A. & SIMON, H. A. (1972). *Human problem solving.* Prentice Hall Inc., Englewood Cliffs, New Jersey.

NISBETT, R. E. & WILSON, T. D. (1979). Telling more than we can know: verbal reports on mental processes. *Psychological Review,* 84:231–259.

PATIL, R. S. (1988). Artificial intelligence techniques for diagnostic reasoning in medicine. In Shrobe, H. E., editor, *Exploring Artificial Intelligence: Survey Talks from the National Conferences on Artificial Intelligence,* pages 347–379. Morgan Kaufmann, San Mateo, California.

POST, W. M., KOSTER, R. W., ZOCCA, V., & SRAMEK, M. (1993). Cooperative medical problem solving. In Andreassen, S., Engelbrecht, R., & Wyatt, J., editors, *Artificial Intelligence in Medicine, Proceedings of the 4th Conference on Artificial Intelligence in Medicine Europe,* pages 259–270. IOS Press, Amsterdam.

RILEY, M. S., GREENO, J. G., & HELLER, J. I. (1983). Development of children's problem-solving ability in arithmetic. In Ginsburg, H. P., editor, *The development of mathematical thinking,* pages 153–196. Academic Press, New York.

SANDBERG, J. A. C., BREUKER, J. A., & WINKELS, R. G. F. (1988). Research on help-systems: Empirical study and model construction. In Kodratoff, Y., editor, *Proceedings of the European Conference on Artificial Intelligence,* pages 106–111. Pitman Publishing, London.

SANDBERG, J. A. C. & DE RUITER, H. (1985). The solving of simple arithmetic story problems. *Instructional Science,* 14:75–86.

SCHREIBER, A. T., WIELINGA, B. J., & BREUKER, J. A., editors (1993). *KADS: A principled approach to knowledge-based system development.* Academic Press, London.

TITCHENER, E. B. (1929). *Systematic psychology: prolegomena.* Macmillan, New York.

VAN DAALEN-KAPTEIJNS, M. M. & ELSHOUT-MOHR, M. (1981). The acquisition of word meanings as a cognitive learning process. *Journal of Verbal Learning and Verbal Behavior*, 20:386–399.

VAN HARMELEN, F. & BALDER, J. R. (1992). (ML)^2: a formal language for KADS models of expertise. *Knowledge Acquisition*, 4(1):127–161.

VAN SOMEREN, M. W. (1990). What's wrong? Understanding beginners' problems with Prolog. *Instructional Science*, 19(4-5):257–282.

VAN SOMEREN, M. W. & ELSHOUT, J. J. (1985). Het effekt van zelfreflektie op leren probleemoplossen (The effect of self-reflection on learning to solve problems). In Lodewijks, J. G. L. C. & Simons, P. R. J., editors, *Zelfstandig leren*, pages 110–117. Swets en Zeitlinger, Lisse (in Dutch).

WIELINGA, B. J., SCHREIBER, A. T., & BREUKER, J. A. (1992). KADS: A modelling approach to knowledge engineering. *Knowledge Acquisition*, 4(1):5–53.

Index

action protocol, 16, 26, 46
aggregation, 117, 118, 120, 124, 125, 133–136
Ariadna, 17, 18, 27

categorical model, 51, 57, 73, 75, 76
coding form, 121
coding procedures, 44, 117, 121, 124–126, 152
coding scheme, 3, 39, 47, 76, 115, 117–127, 130, 132, 134, 136, 152, 172, 193
completeness, 1, 22, 24, 26, 32, 33, 35, 48, 123, 168
conceptual model, 95
conceptual modelling languages, 81
Conceptual Protocol Modelling Language (CPML), 81, 82, 85, 90, 91, 95–98, 112–114
concurrent verbalization, 22, 25, 33
control knowledge, 98, 106, 108, 113, 114

deterministic models, 75, 113, 132
dialogue observation, 23
dialogues, 24
dimensional model, 51, 74, 76, 134

external memory, 68, 106

intercoder reliability, 44, 46, 117, 119, 126–128, 130, 131, 137, 172

interview, 10, 31, 55, 63, 81, 155, 156, 168
introspection, 22, 25, 26, 29–31, 35, 57

KADS, 82
knowledge based system, 79

long-term memory, 19, 20, 22, 23, 91, 108

observation, 46, 118
observation methods, 13, 15, 16, 23, 26, 29, 30, 33, 39
organization model, 11

Problem Behaviour Graph (PBG), 81, 98, 99, 101, 106
procedural model, 51–56, 58, 62, 63, 73, 80, 81, 118, 126, 131, 159
production rules, 53, 81, 98, 101–105, 107–114, 120, 123, 150, 164
prompting, 18, 23–27, 31, 44, 120
pseudo programming language, 81, 96, 97, 112, 114
psychological model, 37, 39, 49, 53, 54, 62, 64, 68, 69, 72, 74–77, 79, 80, 107, 109, 111, 150, 168, 170, 172, 193

retrospection, 20–22, 24, 26, 35, 48, 167, 168

review, 20, 48

segmentation, 117, 118, 120, 121, 125, 127
selecting problems, 36
selecting subjects, 34–36
structured techniques, 31, 32
synchronization, 33, 34, 37, 122

task analysis, 37, 54, 56–58, 62–69, 72, 73, 75–77, 79, 120, 140, 151, 155, 156, 158, 160, 164, 168, 170, 172

validity, 21, 24, 32, 33, 39, 42, 168

working memory, 19, 20, 22, 23, 30, 33, 34, 37, 56, 65–67, 102–111, 122, 123, 160, 161, 164